Disney for Organ

Disney characters and artwork © Disney Enterprises, Inc.

The following song is the property of:
Bourne Co.
Music Publishers
5 West 37th Street
New York, NY 10018

WHEN YOU WISH UPON A STAR

ISBN 978-1-4584-0520-3

WALT DISNEY MUSIC COMPANY
WONDERLAND MUSIC COMPANY, INC.

DISTRIBUTED BY

HAL•LEONARD®
CORPORATION
7777 W. BLUEMOUND RD. P.O. BOX 13819 MILWAUKEE, WI 53213

Visit Hal Leonard Online at
www.halleonard.com

Be Our Guest
from Walt Disney's BEAUTY AND THE BEAST

Electronic Organs

Upper: Accordion Preset
Lower: Strings, low brass
Pedal: Bass 16
Vib./Trem.: On, fast

Drawbar Organs

Upper: 80 4800 002
Lower: (00) 7334 011
Pedal: 53
Vib./Trem.: On, fast

Lyrics by HOWARD ASHMAN
Music by ALAN MENKEN

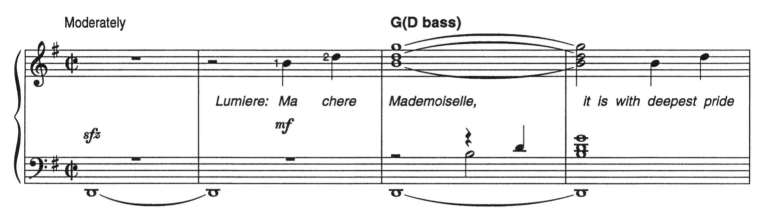

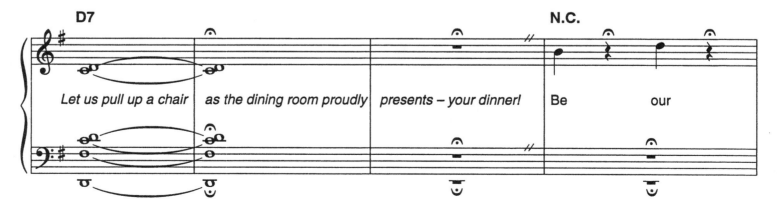

Jauntily

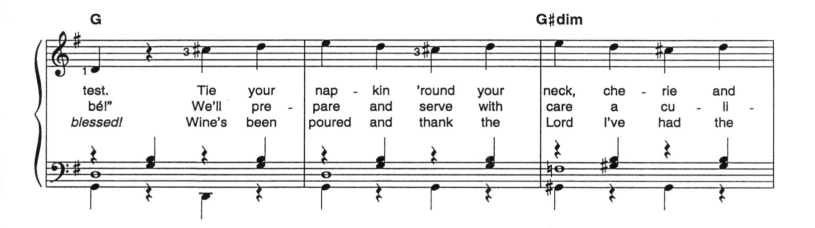

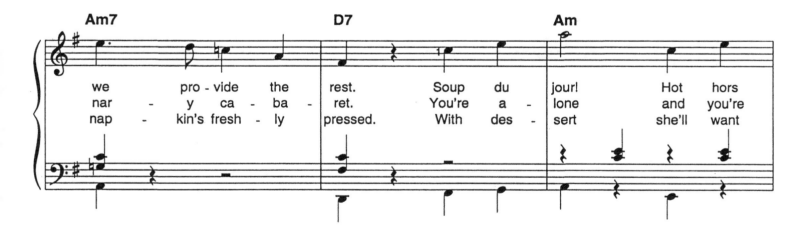

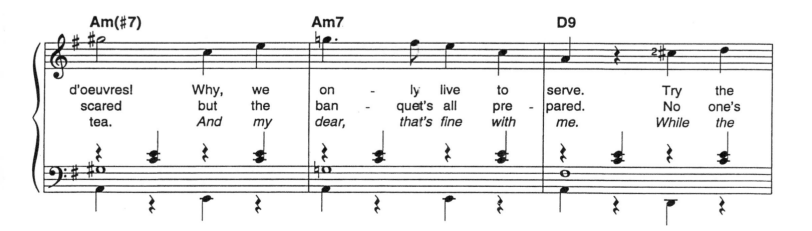

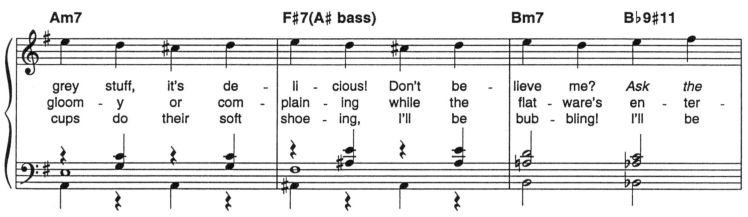

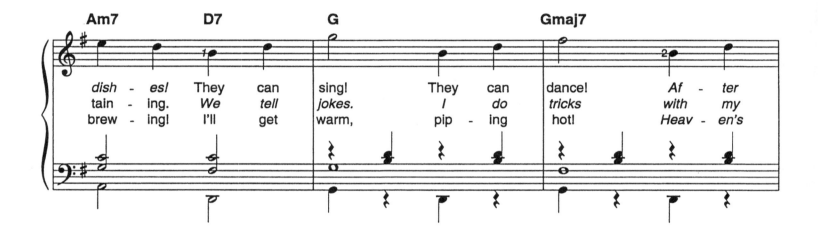

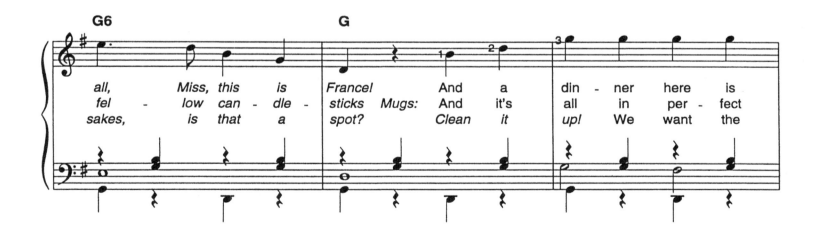

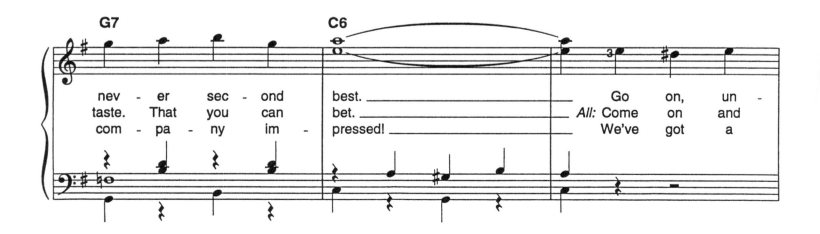

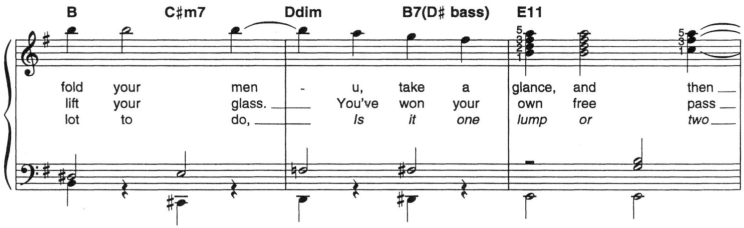

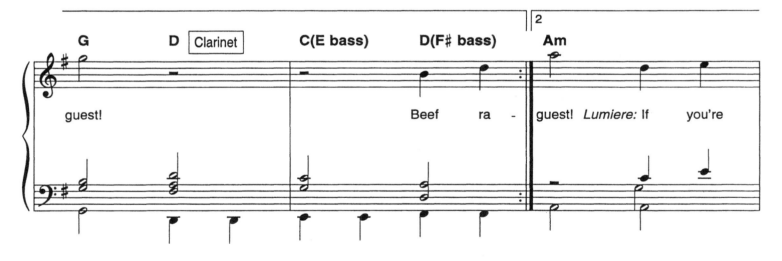

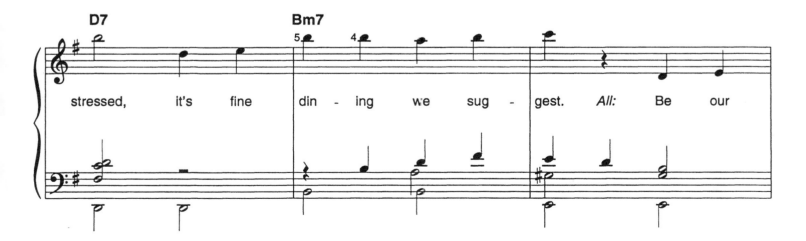

Am7 **D7** **G** **B7** [Violin]

guest! Be our guest! Be our guest!

[Soft Strings]

Slower, melancholy

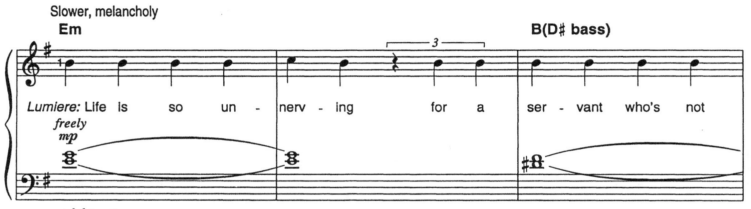

Em **B(D♯ bass)**

Lumiere: Life is so un - nerv - ing for a ser - vant who's not

freely
mp

pedal tacet

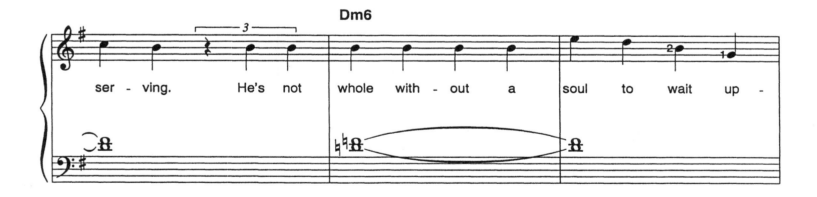

Dm6

ser - ving. He's not whole with - out a soul to wait up -

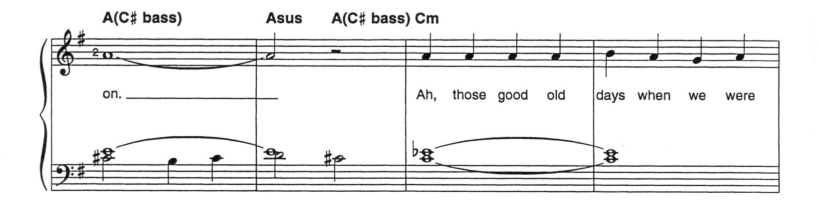

A(C♯ bass) **Asus** **A(C♯ bass) Cm**

on. _____ Ah, those good old days when we were

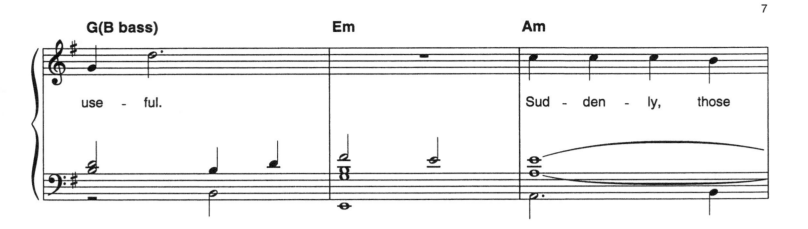

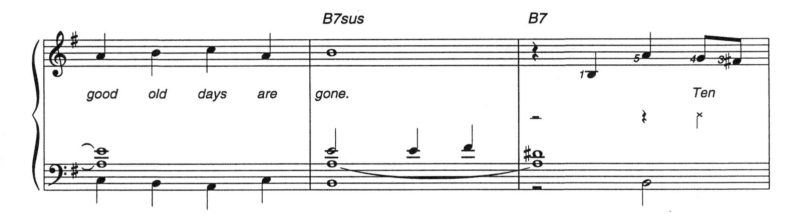

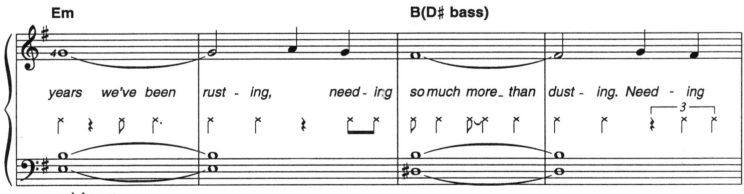

pedal tacet

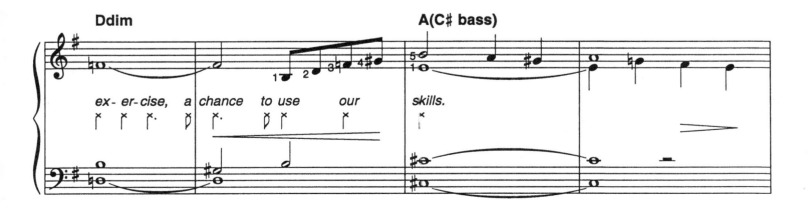

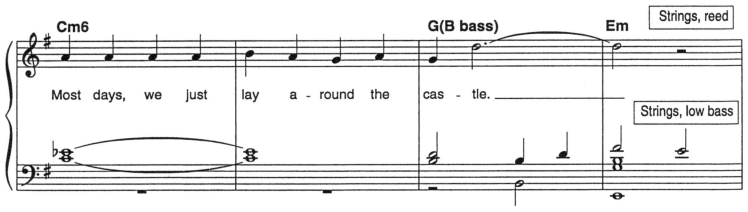

Cm6 — Most days, we just lay a-round the cas-tle. _____ G(B bass) Em

Strings, reed

Strings, low bass

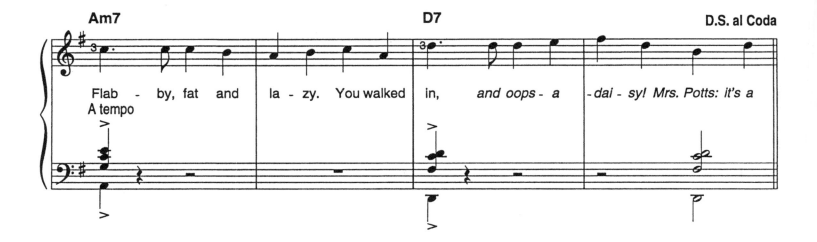

Am7 — Flab-by, fat and la-zy. You walked in, *and oops-a -dai-sy!* Mrs. Potts: it's a D7 D.S. al Coda

A tempo

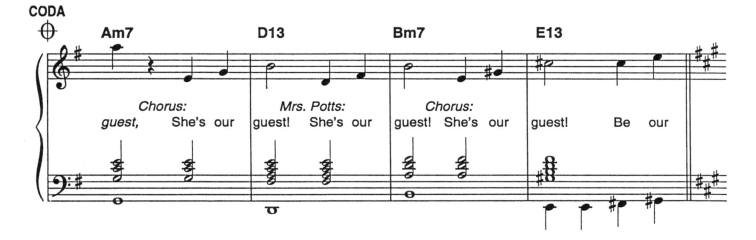

CODA

Am7 — *Chorus:* guest, She's our D13 — *Mrs. Potts:* guest! She's our Bm7 — *Chorus:* guest! She's our E13 — guest! Be our

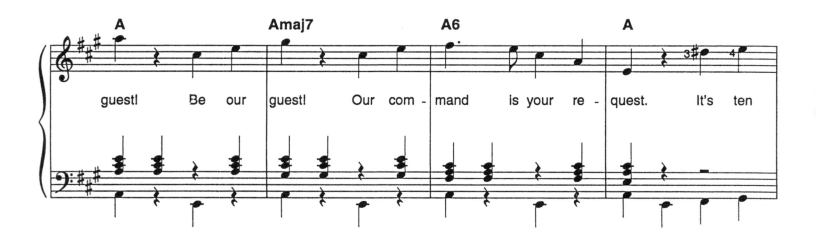

A — guest! Be our Amaj7 — guest! Our com-mand A6 — is your re-quest. A — It's ten

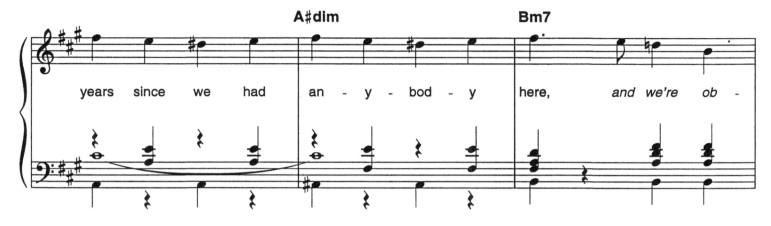

years since we had an - y - bod - y here, *and we're ob -*

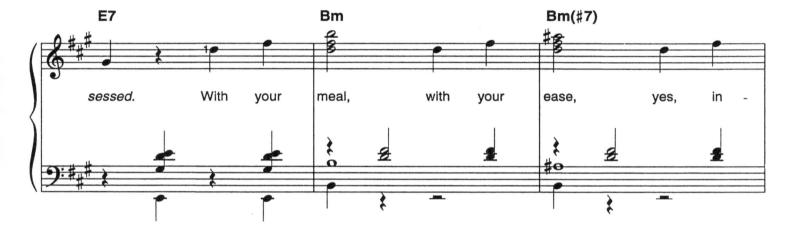

sessed. With your meal, with your ease, yes, in -

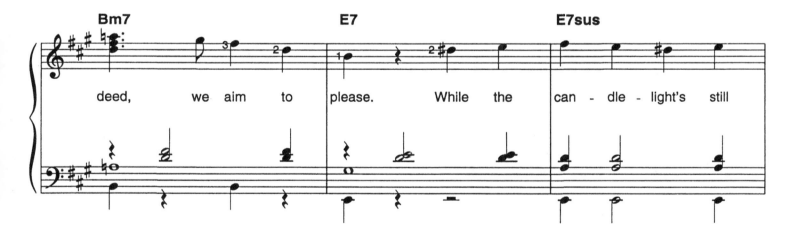

deed, we aim to please. While the can - dle - light's still

glow - ing let us help you, we'll keep go - ing course by

molto rit.

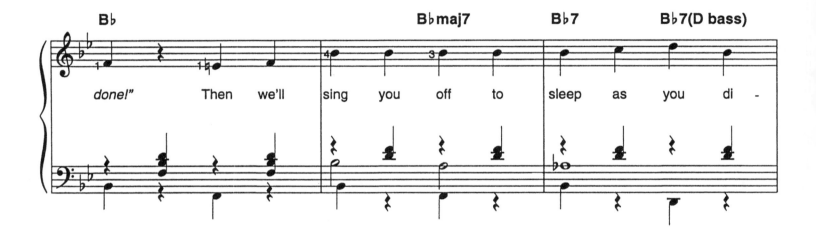

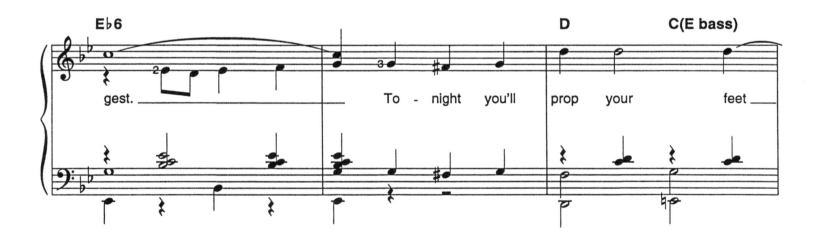

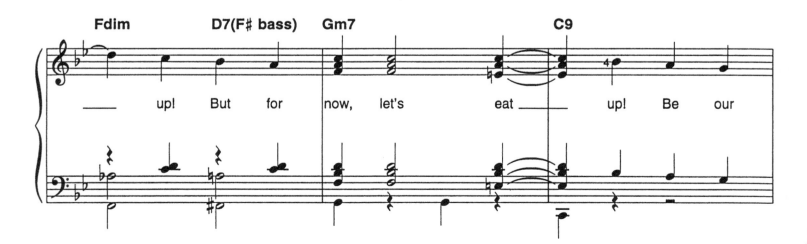

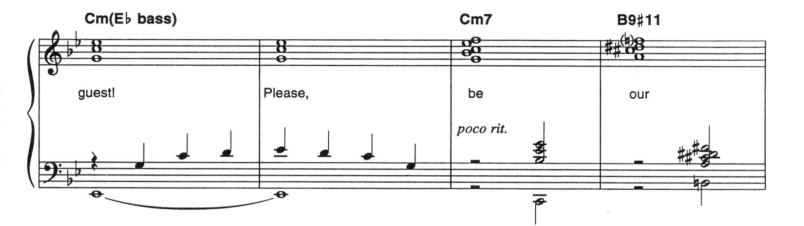

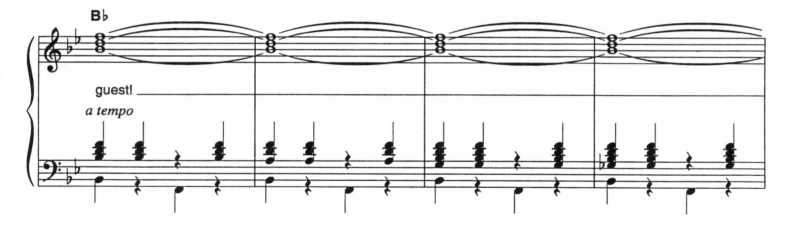

Beauty and the Beast
from Walt Disney's BEAUTY AND THE BEAST

Electronic Organs

Upper: Flute 4'
Lower: Strings
Pedal: Bass 8' or
    Elec. bass (soft)
Vib./Trem.: On, Fast

Drawbar Organs

Upper: 60 0608 008
Lower: (00) 6500 001
Pedal: 05
Vib./Trem.: On, fast

Lyrics by HOWARD ASHMAN
Music by ALAN MENKEN

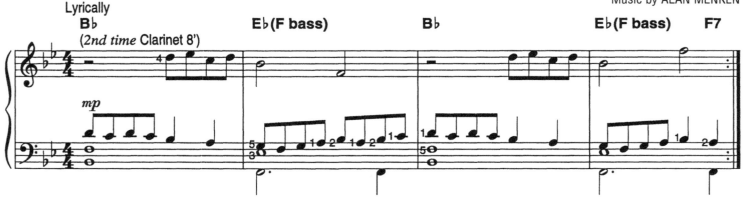

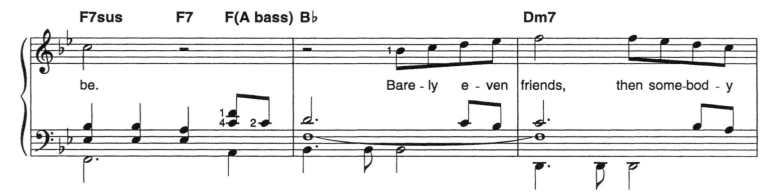

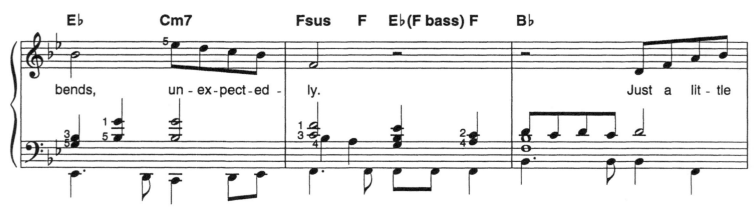

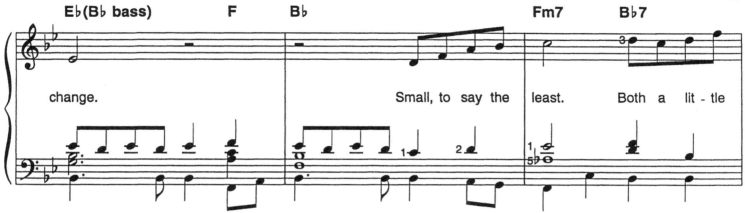

change.   Small, to say the   least.   Both a   lit - tle

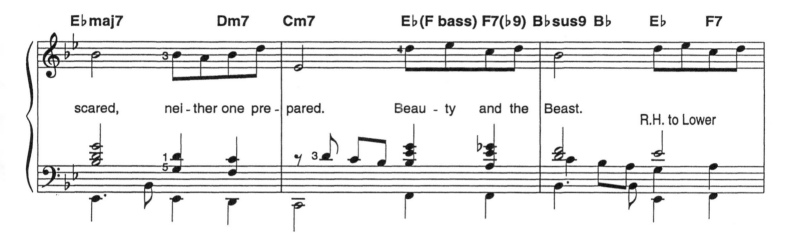

scared,   nei - ther one pre - pared.   Beau - ty   and the   Beast.

R.H. to Lower

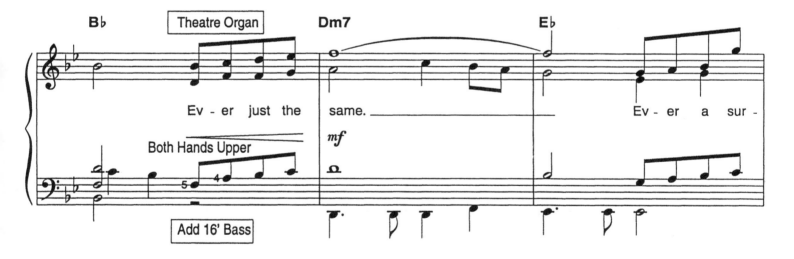

Ev - er   just the   same. _____   Ev - er   a   sur -

Both Hands Upper

mf

Add 16' Bass

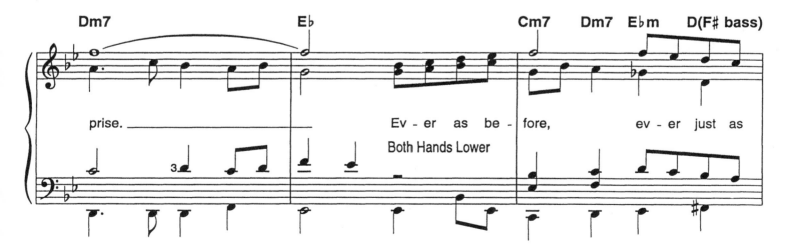

prise. _____   Ev - er as   be - fore,   ev - er   just as

Both Hands Lower

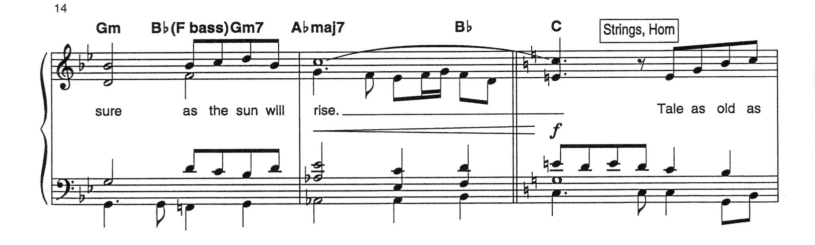

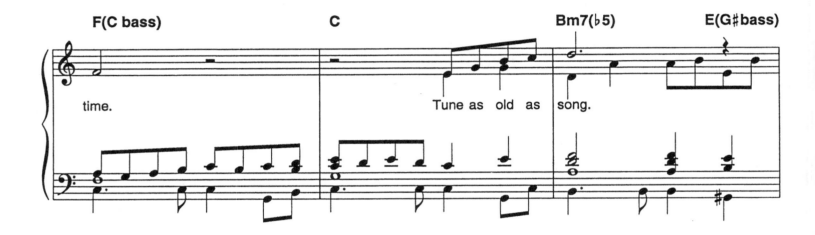

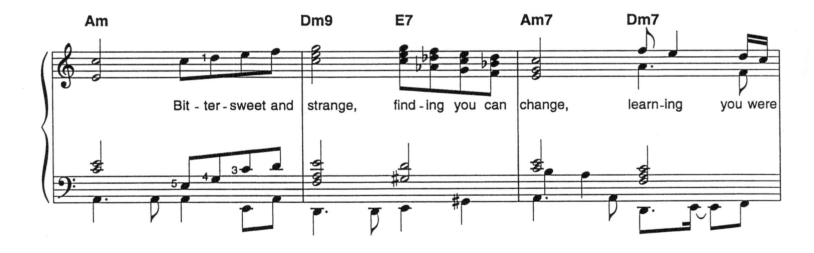

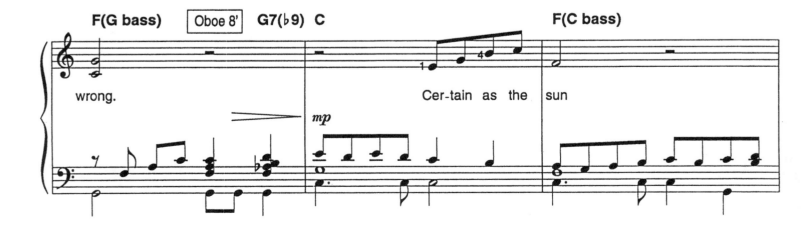

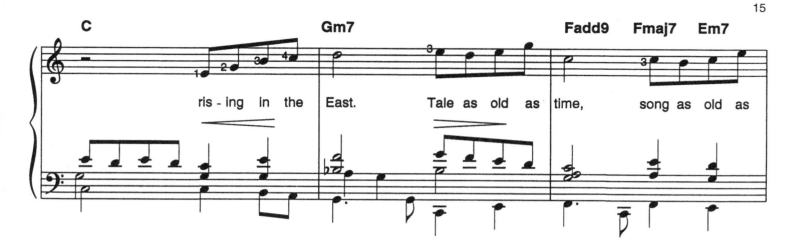

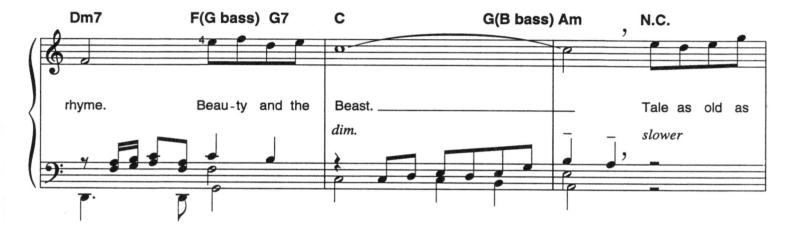

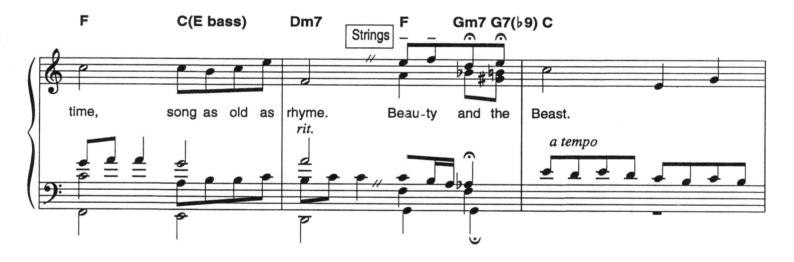

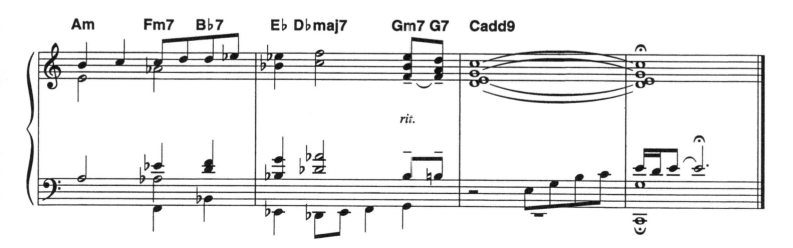

Can You Feel the Love Tonight
from Walt Disney Pictures' THE LION KING

Electronic Organs
Upper: Flute (or Tibia) 4'
  Clarinet 8'
Lower: Strings 8', 4'
Pedal: 16', 8'
Vib./Trem.: On, Fast

Drawbar Organs
Upper: 53 5864 101
Lower: (00) 7104 000
Pedal: 35
Vib./Trem.: On, Fast

Music by ELTON JOHN
Lyrics by TIM RICE

Freely, in a narrative manner
(Auto Rhythm off)

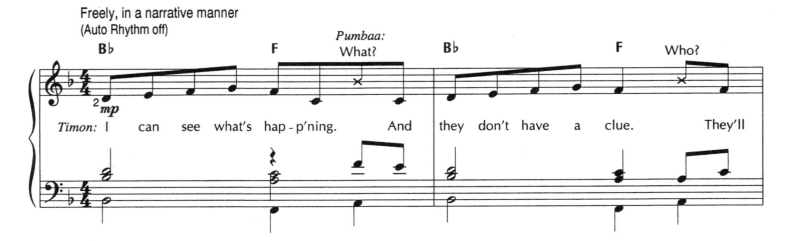

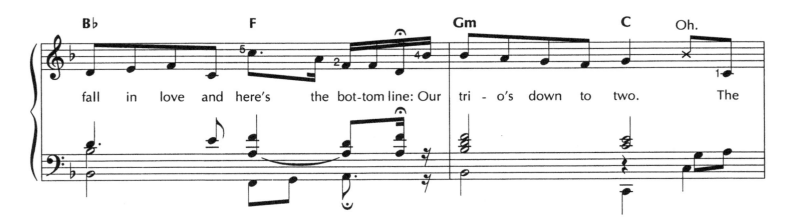

with all this ro - man - tic at-mos-phere, __ dis - as - ter's in the

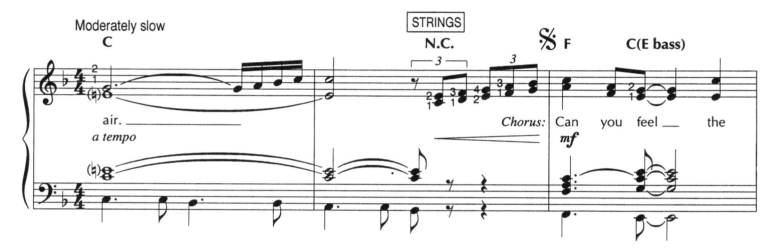

air. __ *Chorus:* Can you feel __ the

love to - night, __ the peace the eve - ning brings? The

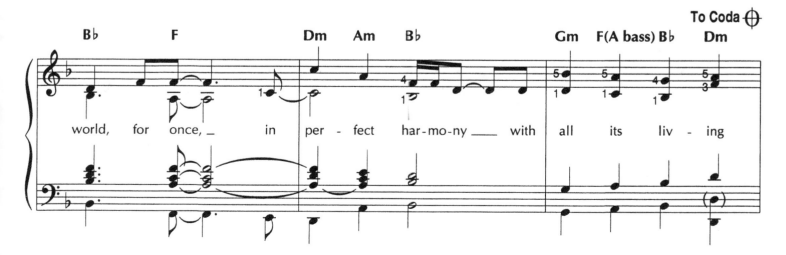

world, for once, __ in per - fect har-mo-ny __ with all its liv - ing

things. *Simba:* So man-y things to tell her, but how to make her see the

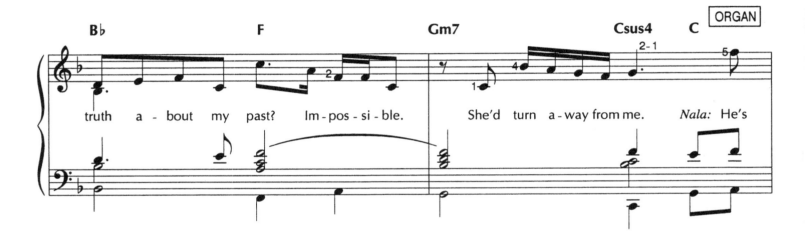

truth a-bout my past? Im-pos-si-ble. She'd turn a-way from me. *Nala:* He's

hold-ing back, he's hid-ing. But what? I can't de-cide. Why

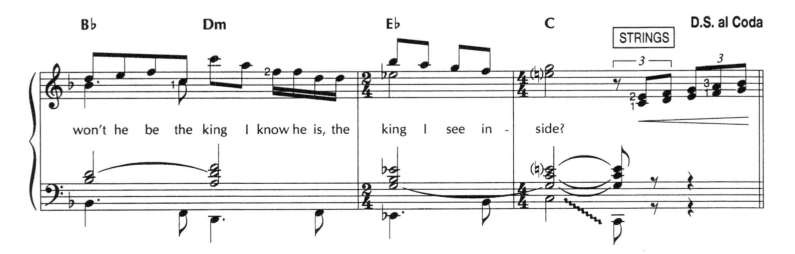

won't he be the king I know he is, the king I see in-side?

CODA

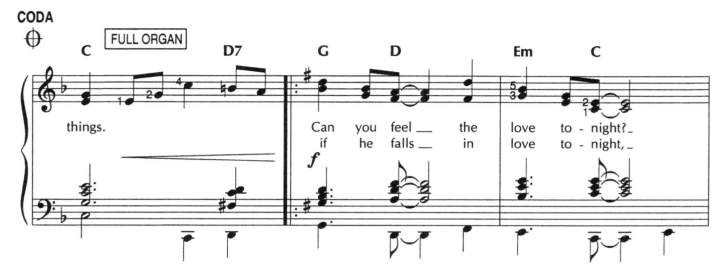

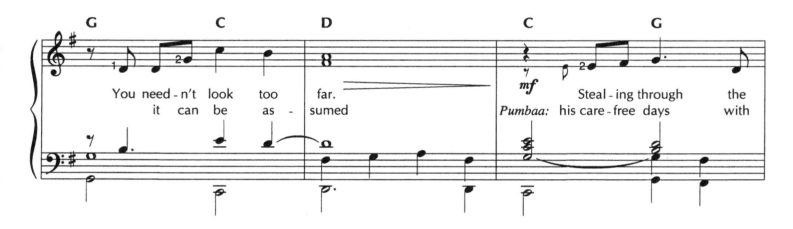

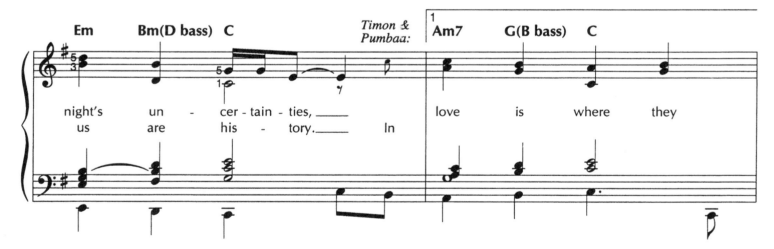

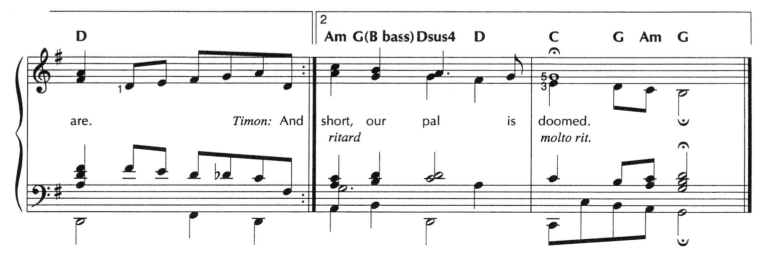

Circle of Life
from Walt Disney Pictures' THE LION KING

Electronic Organs
Upper: Flutes (or Tibias) 8', 4'
      Horn 8'
Lower: Melodia 8', Reed 8'
Pedal: String Bass
Vib./Trem.: On, Fast

Drawbar Organs
Upper: 53 6606 000
Lower: (00) 7400 011
Pedal: String Bass
Vib./Trem.: On, Fast

Music by ELTON JOHN
Lyrics by TIM RICE

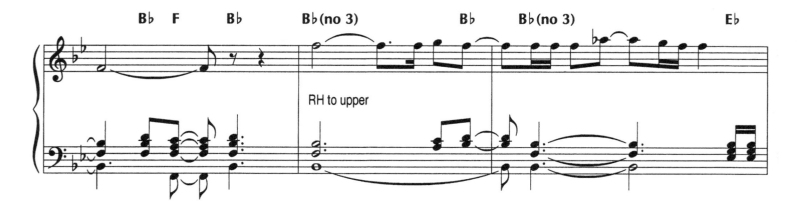

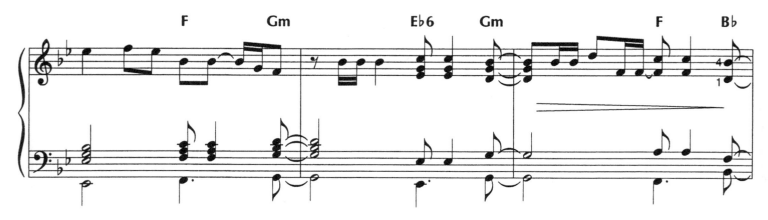

Same tempo, gently and rhythmically

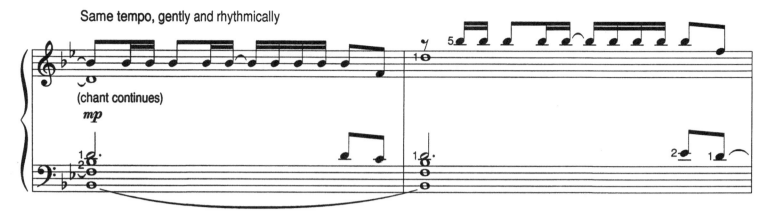

(chant continues)

mp

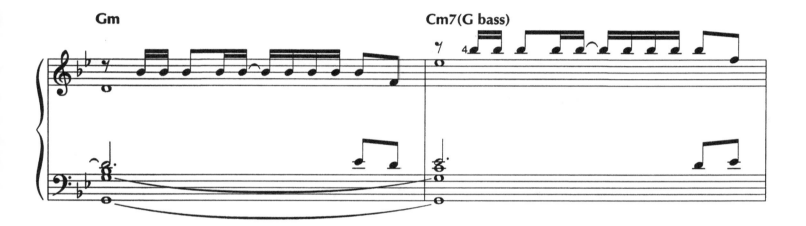

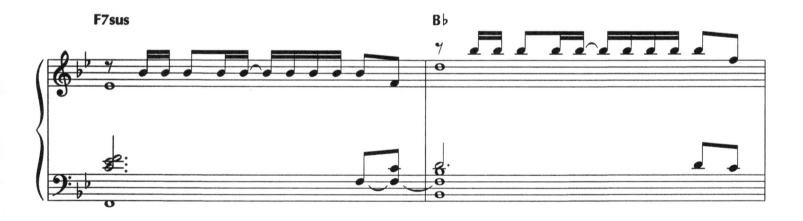

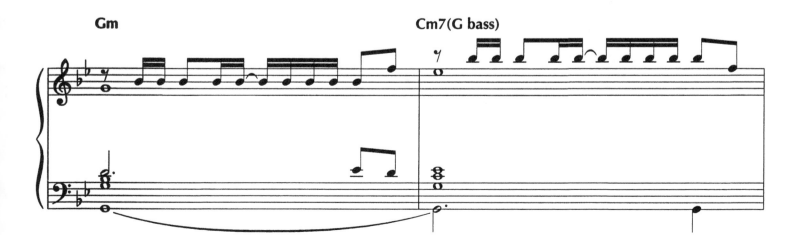

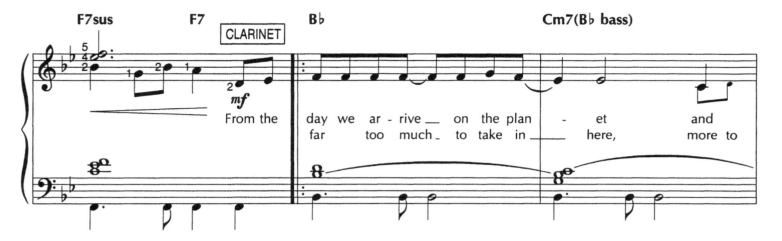

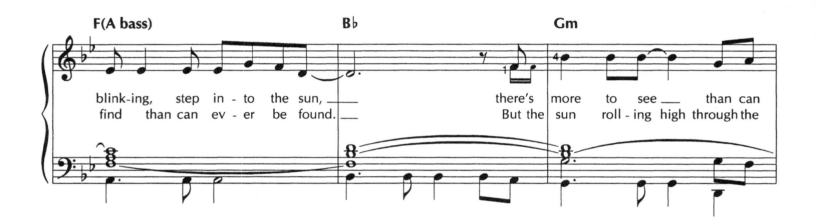

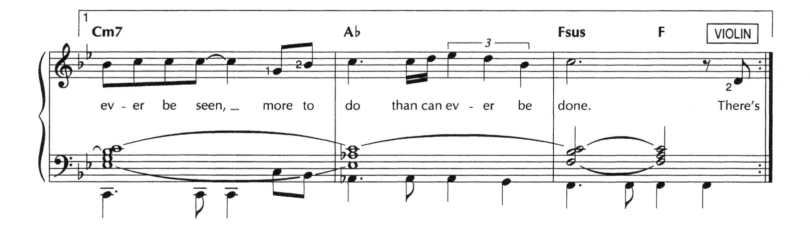

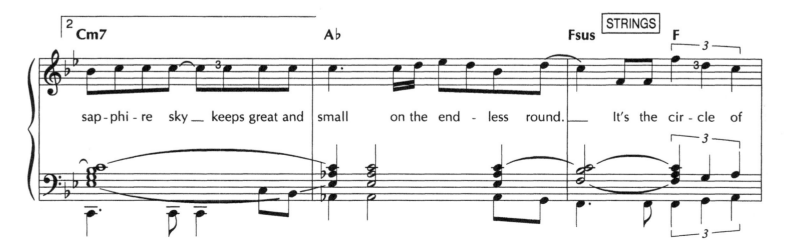

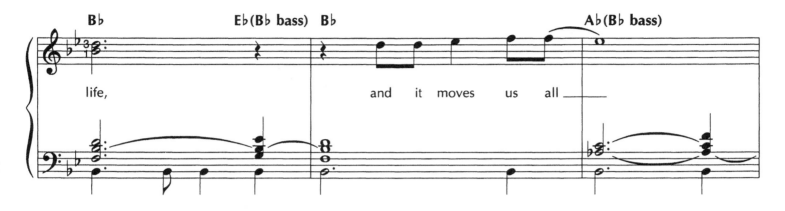

life, and it moves us all ___

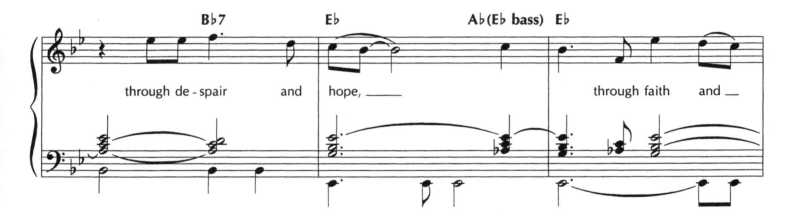

through de - spair and hope, ___ through faith and ___

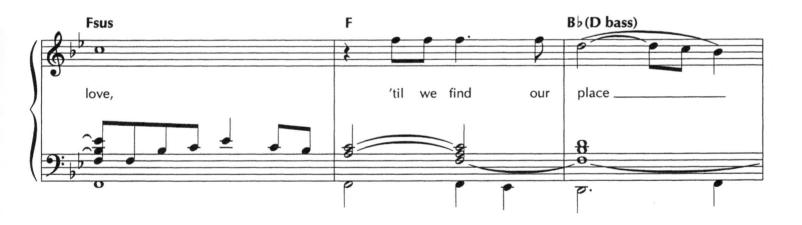

love, 'til we find our place ___

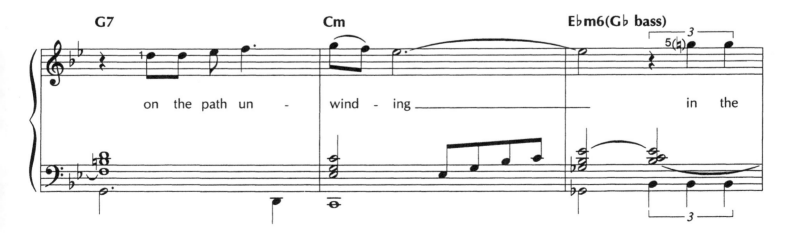

on the path un - wind - ing ___ in the

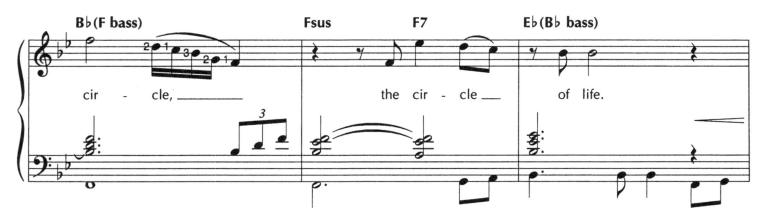

cir - cle, _____ the cir - cle ___ of life.

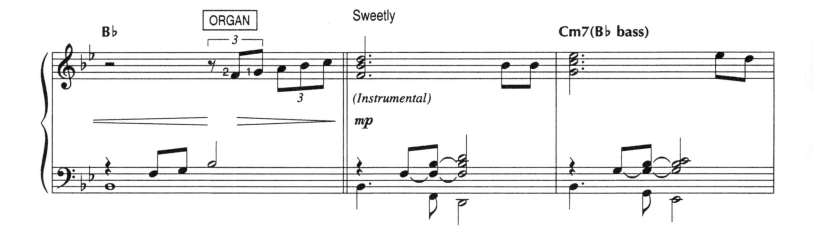

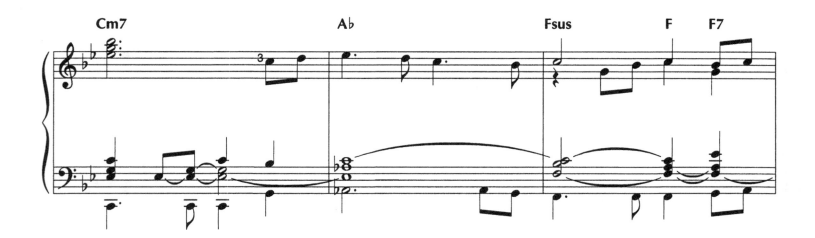

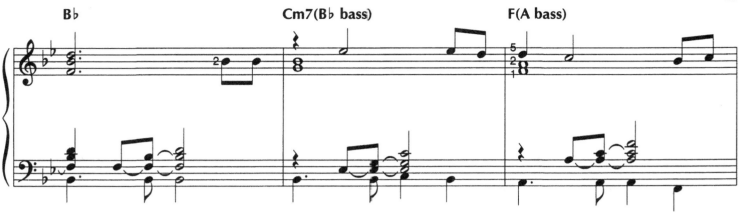

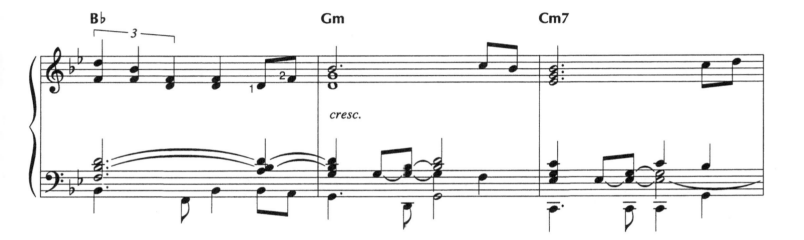

ADD VIOLIN

It's the cir - cle of life,

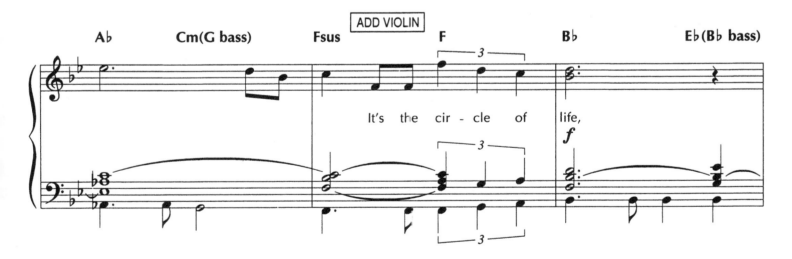

and it moves us all _____ through de - spair and ___

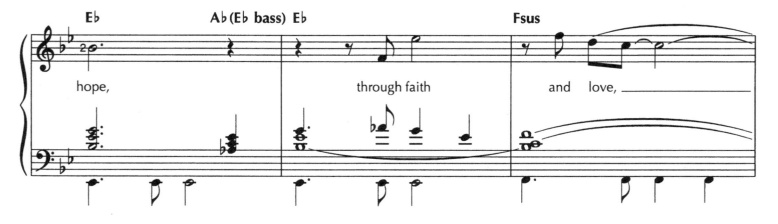

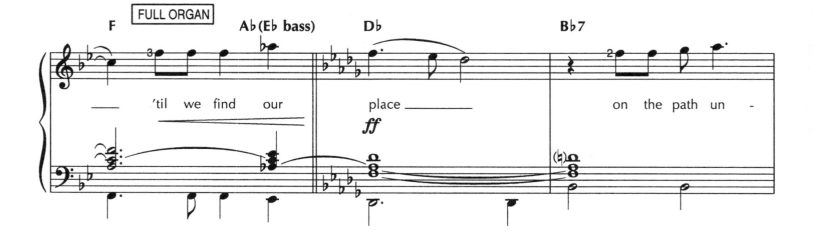

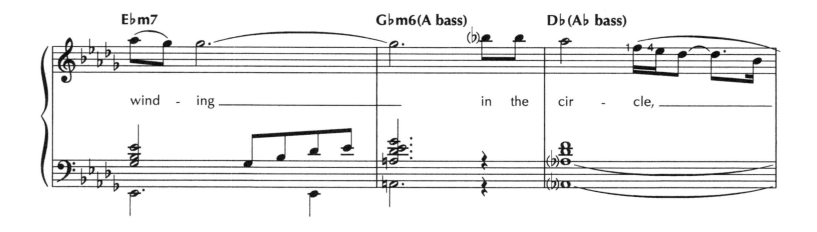

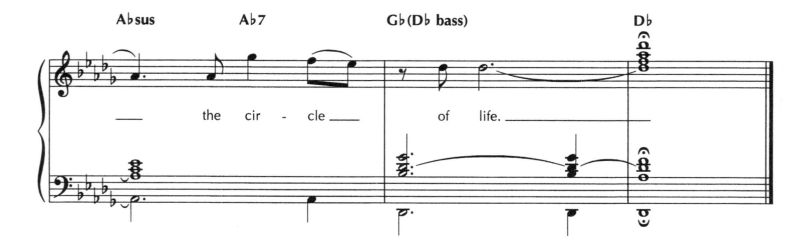

A Dream Is a Wish Your Heart Makes

from Walt Disney's CINDERELLA

Electronic and Pipe Organs

Upper: Flutes (or Tibias) 16', 8', 4', 2'
         Oboe 8', String 4'
Lower: Diapason 8'
         Flute 4'
Pedal: 16', 8' Sustain
Trem: On — Full
Automatic Rhythm: Swing or Ballad

Drawbar Organs

Upper: 60 5806 660 (00)
Lower: (00) 6534 333 (0)
Pedal: 5 (0) 5 (0) (Spinet 5)
Vibrato: On — Full
Automatic Rhythm: Swing or Ballad

Words and Music by MACK DAVID,
AL HOFFMAN and JERRY LIVINGSTON

Moderately

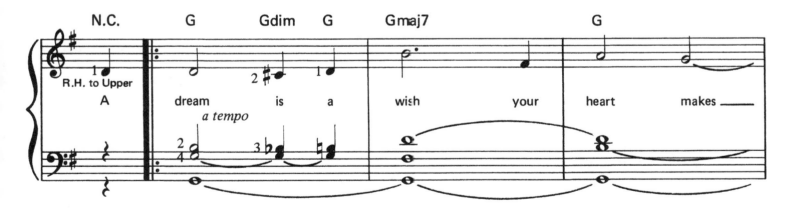

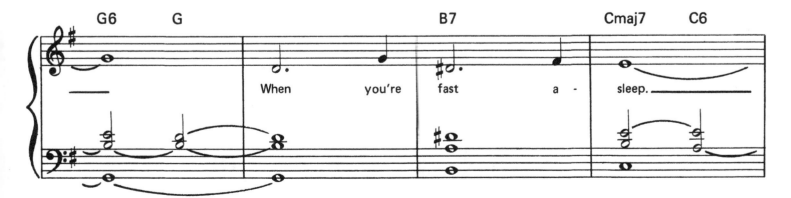

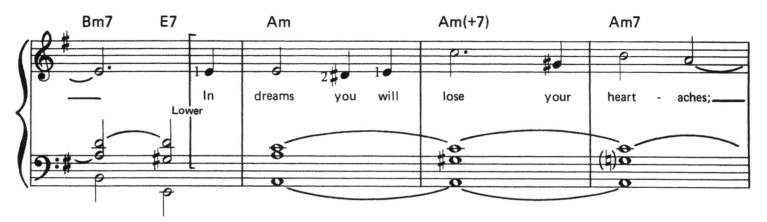

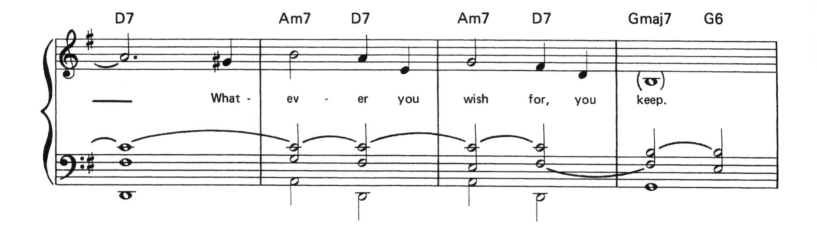

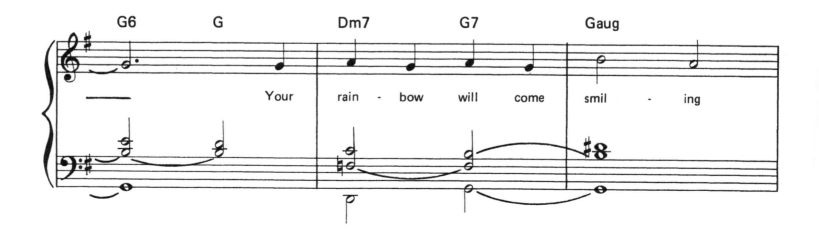

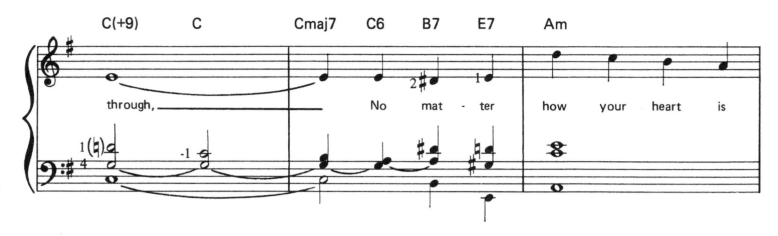

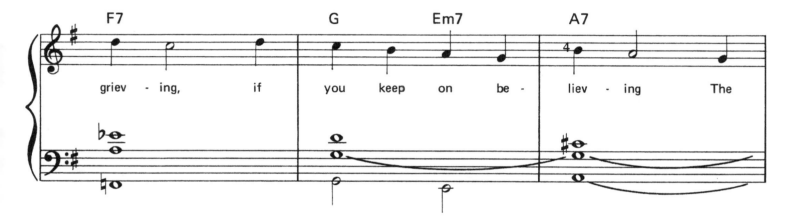

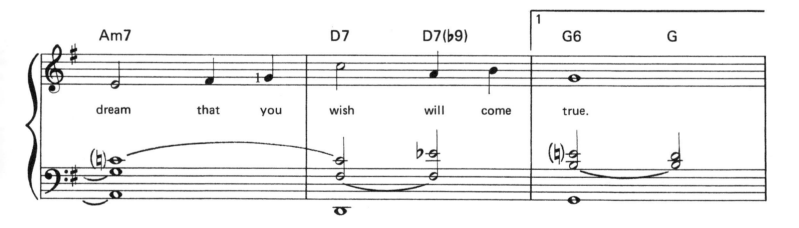

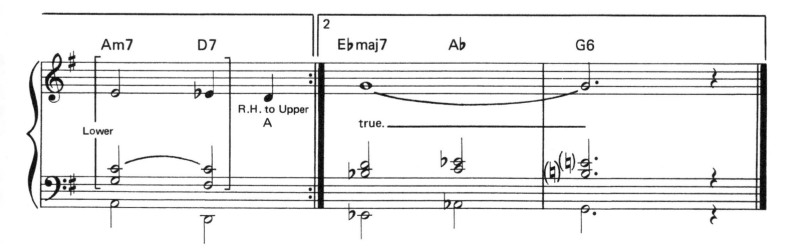

Colors of the Wind
from Walt Disney's POCAHONTAS

Electronic Organs
Upper: Flute (or Tibia) 16', 4'
       Trombone
       Trumpet
Lower: Flute 8', 4'
       String 8'
Pedal: 16', 8'
Vib./Trem.: On, Fast

Drawbar Organs
Upper: 83 0313 003
Lower: (00) 6303 002
Pedal: 35
Vib./Trem.: On, Fast

Music by ALAN MENKEN
Lyrics by STEPHEN SCHWARTZ

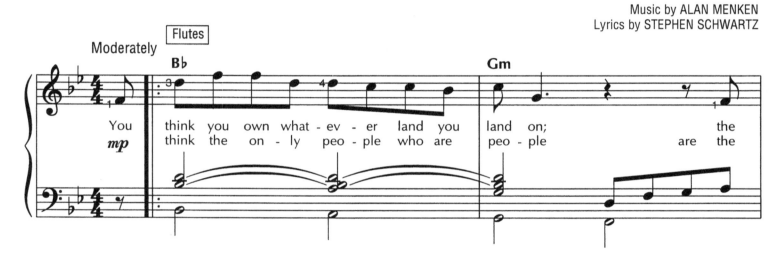

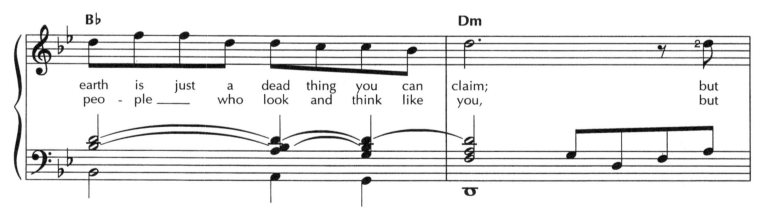

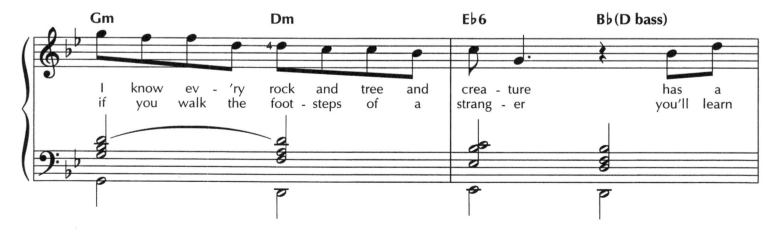

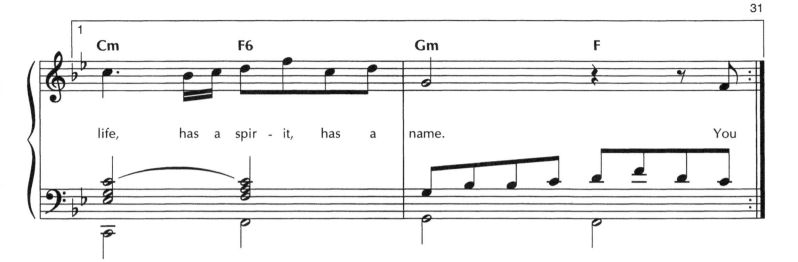

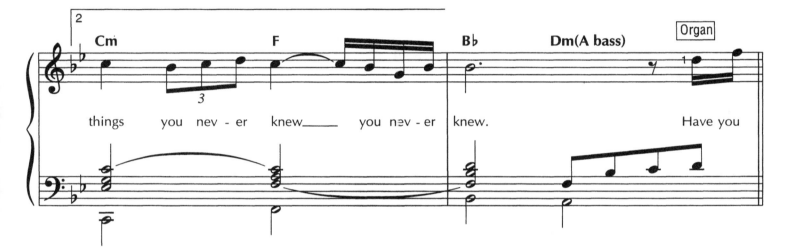

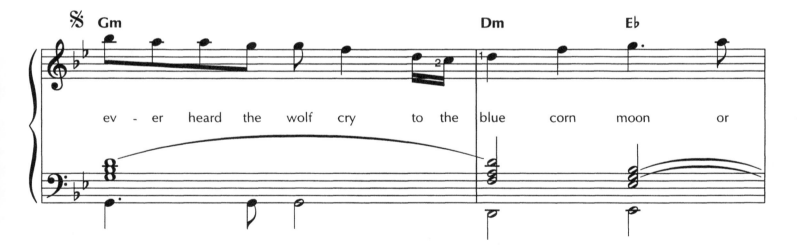

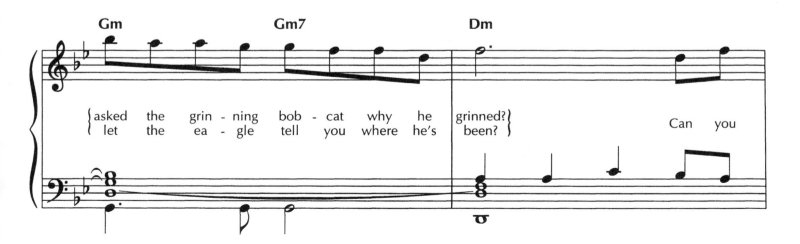

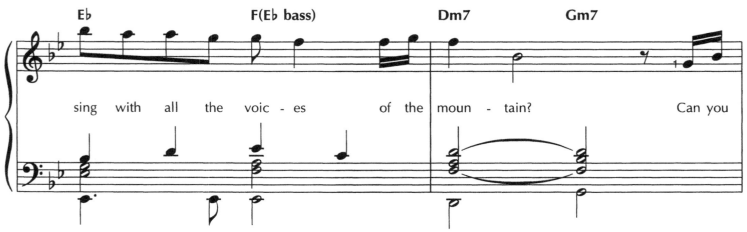

Eb   F(Eb bass)   Dm7   Gm7

sing with all the voic - es   of the moun - tain?   Can you

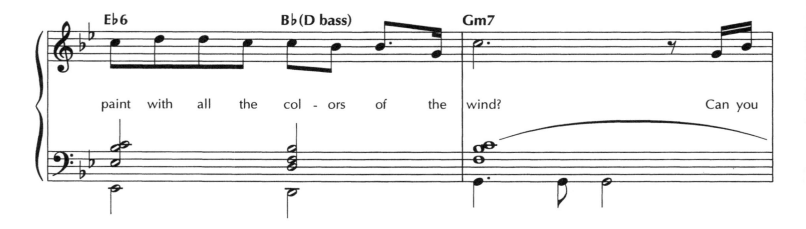

Eb6   Bb(D bass)   Gm7

paint with all the col - ors of the wind?   Can you

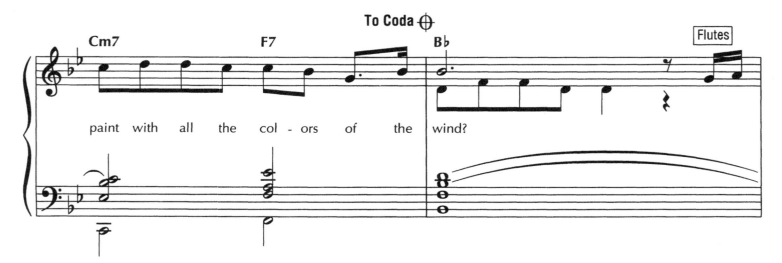

To Coda ⊕

Cm7   F7   Bb   Flutes

paint with all the col - ors of the wind?

Gm   F   Bb   F(A bass)

Come   run the hid - den pine trails of the
rain - storm and the riv - er are my

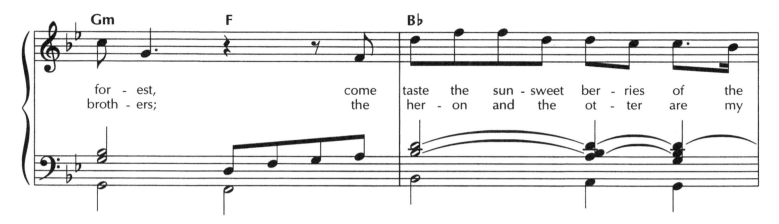

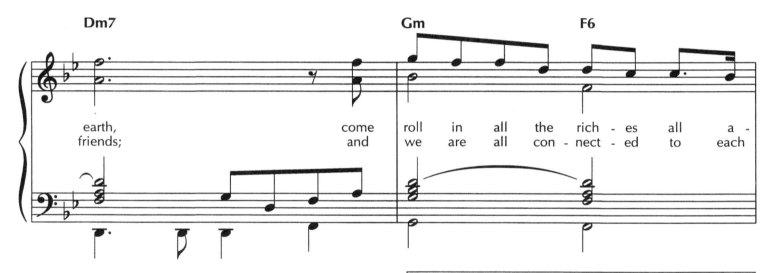

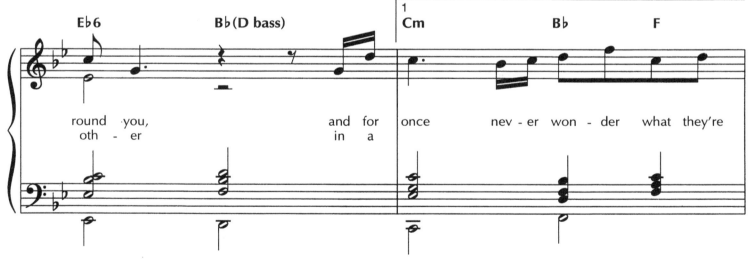

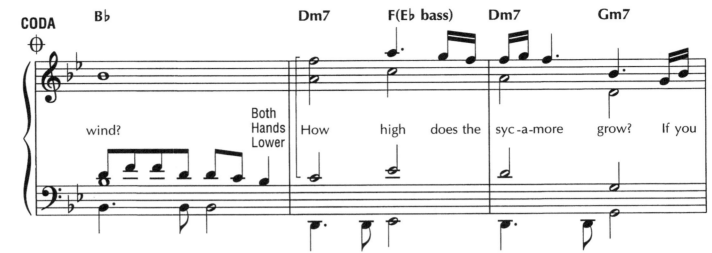

CODA

Bb   **Dm7**   **F(Eb bass)**   **Dm7**   **Gm7**

wind?

Both
Hands
Lower

How high does the syc-a-more grow? If you

Abmaj7   **Eb(F bass)**   **F6**   **Eb(F bass)**   **F**

cut it down _____ then you'll nev - er know._____ And you'll

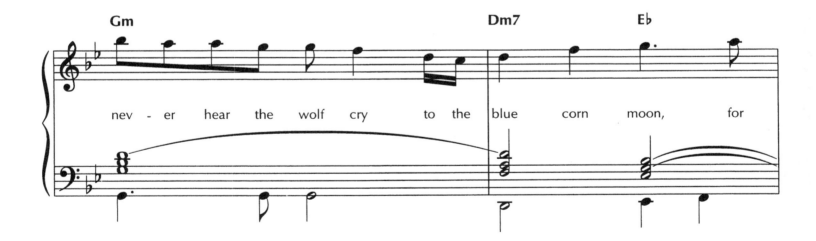

Gm   **Dm7**   **Eb**

nev - er hear the wolf cry to the blue corn moon, for

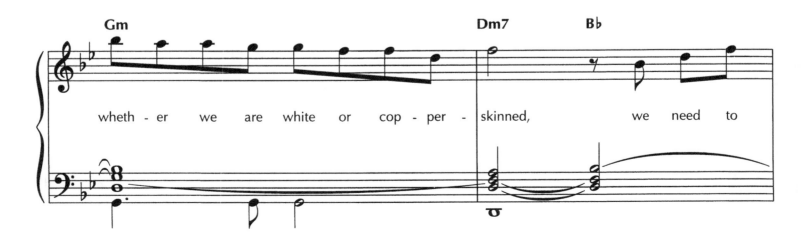

Gm   **Dm7**   **Bb**

wheth - er we are white or cop - per - skinned, we need to

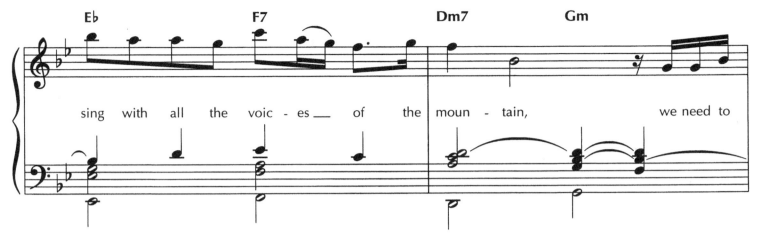

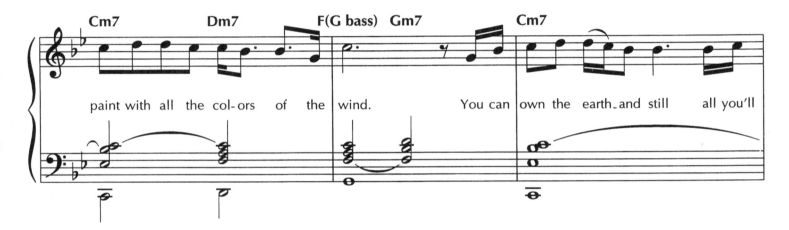

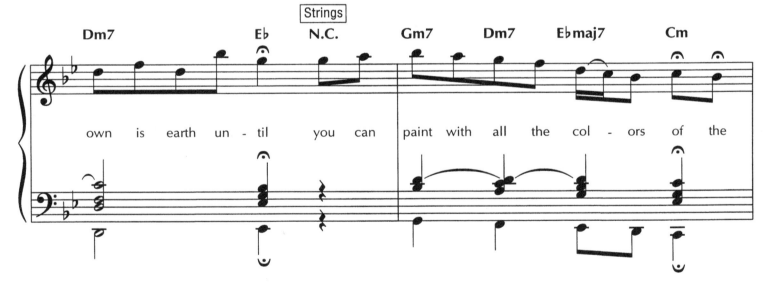

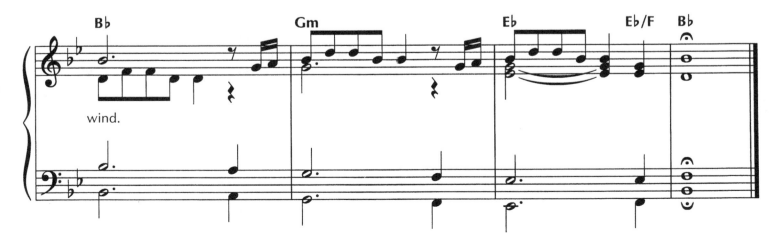

Friend Like Me
from Walt Disney's ALADDIN

Electronic Organs
Upper: Flute (or Tibia) 16', 4'
      Trombone
      Trumpet
Lower: Flute 8', 4'
      String 8'
Pedal: 16', 8'
Vib./Trem.: On, Fast

Drawbar Organs
Upper: 83 0313 003
Lower: (00) 6303 002
Pedal: 35
Vib./Trem.: On, Fast

Lyrics by HOWARD ASHMAN
Music by ALAN MENKEN

Bright two-beat

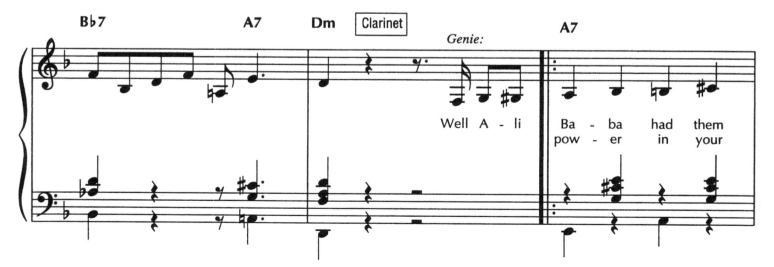

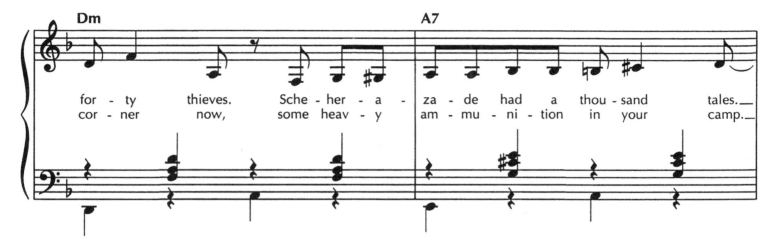

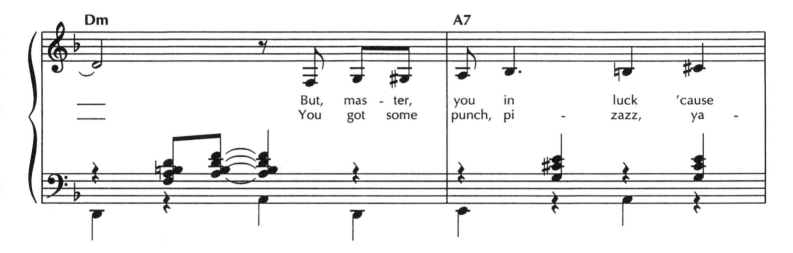

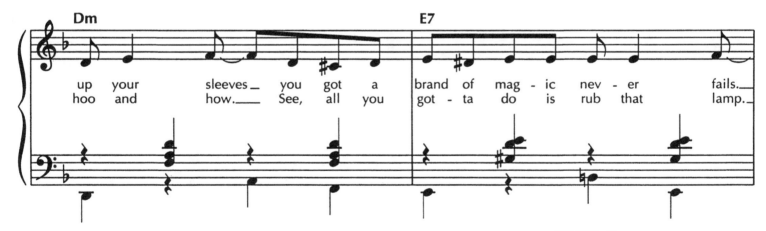

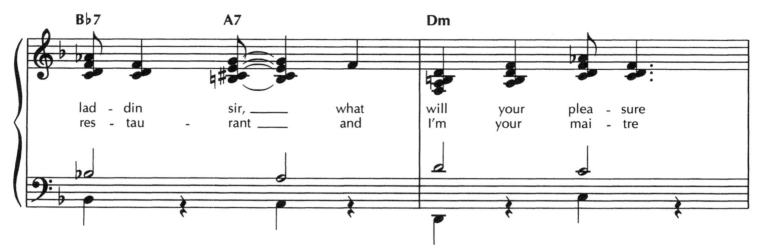

lad - din sir, _____ what will your plea - sure
res - tau - rant _____ what and I'm your mai - tre

be? Let me take your or - der,
d'. C' - mon whis - per what it

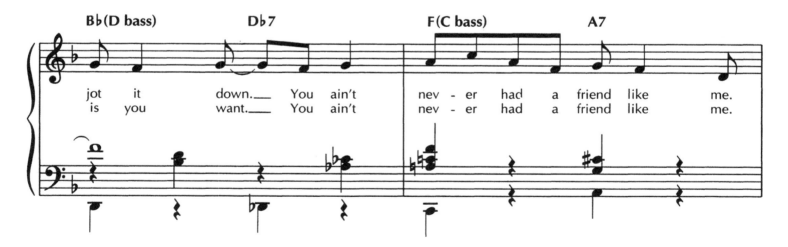

jot it down._____ You ain't nev - er had a friend like me.
is you want._____ You ain't nev - er had a friend like me.

No no _____ no. Yes, sir, we pride our - selves on

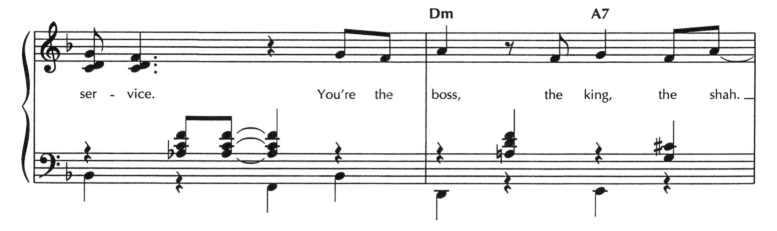

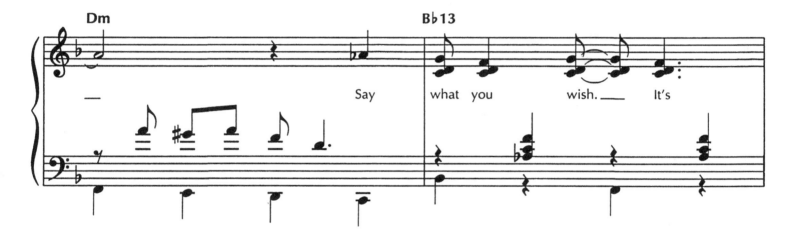

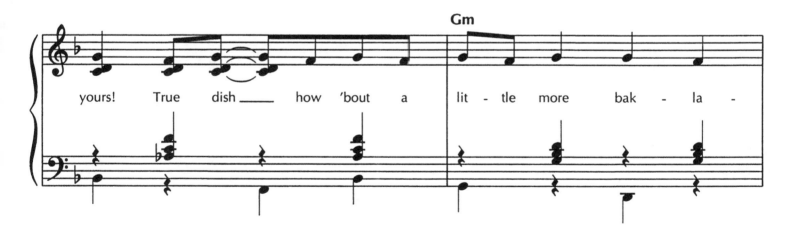

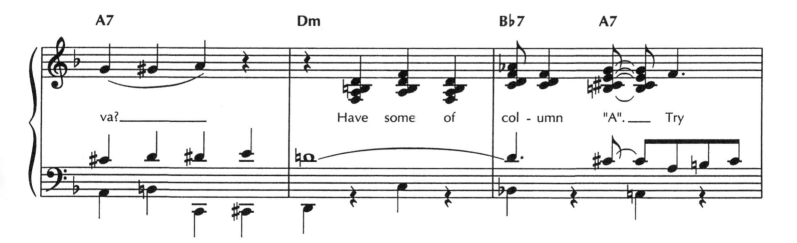

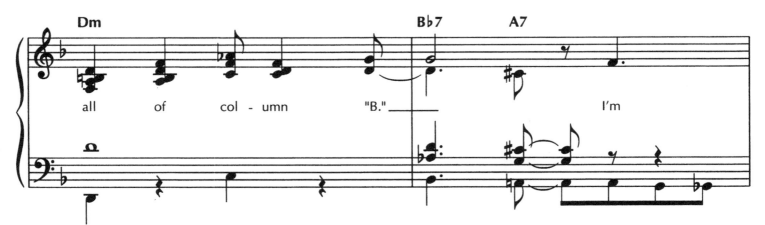

all of col - umn "B."___ I'm

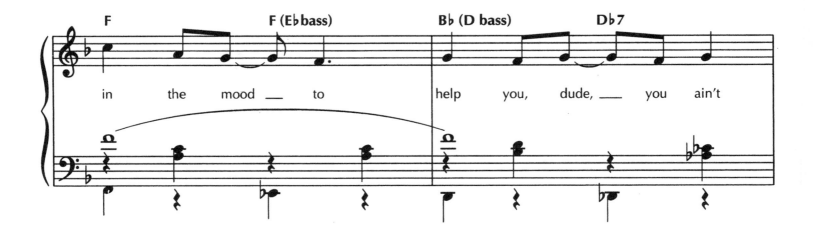

in the mood ___ to help you, dude, ___ you ain't

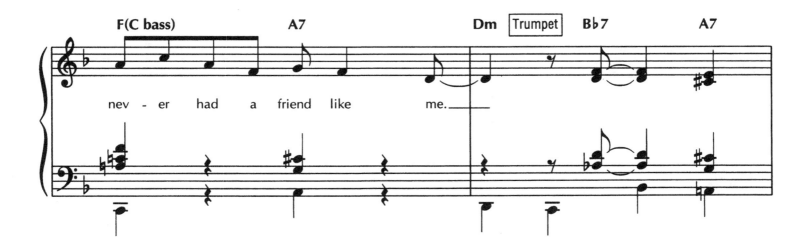

nev - er had a friend like me. ___

Wa - ah - ah. ___ Oh my. ___ Wa - ah - ah. ___

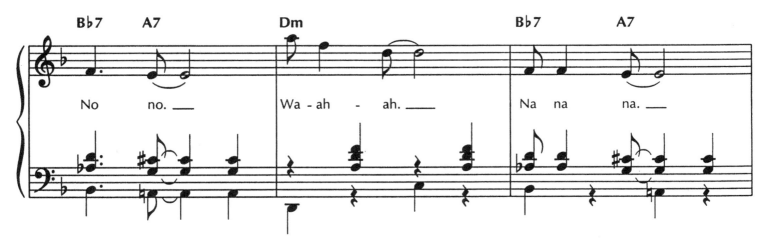

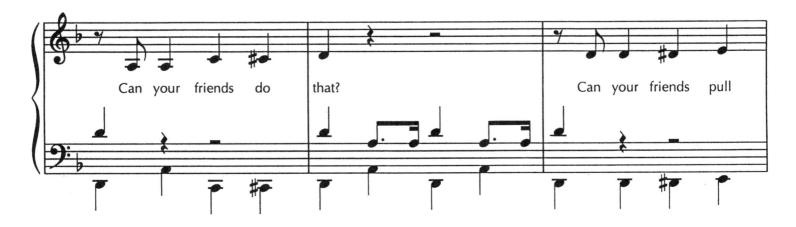

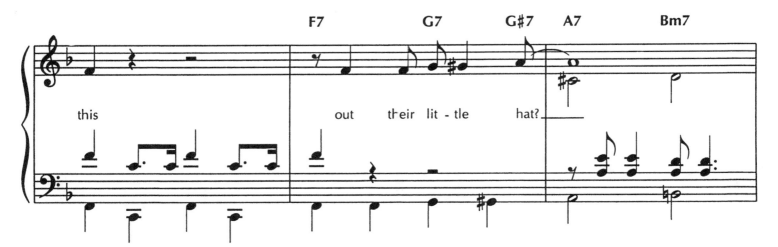

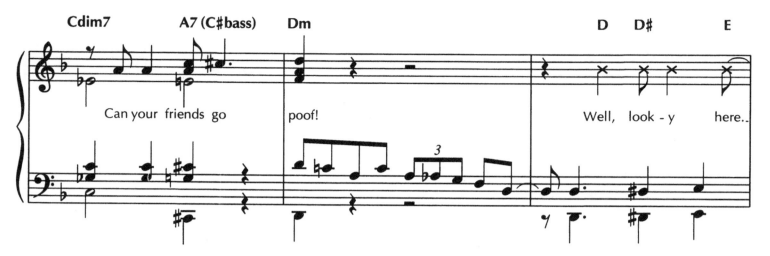

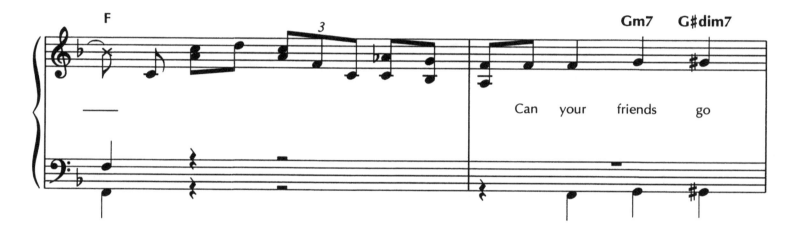

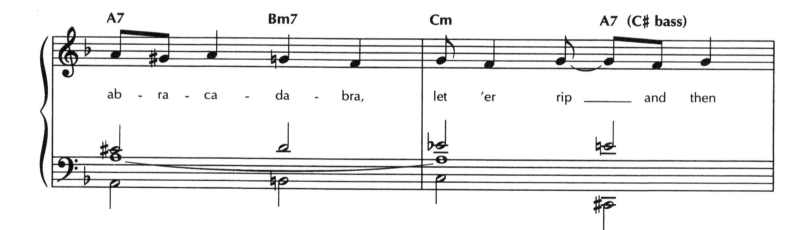

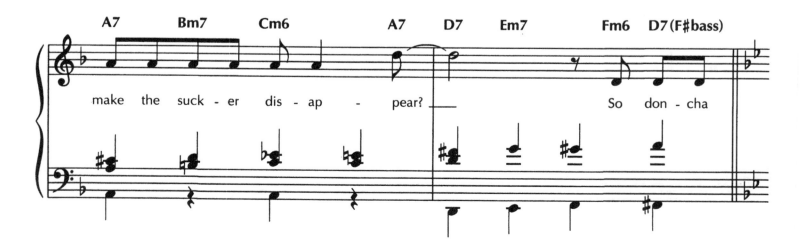

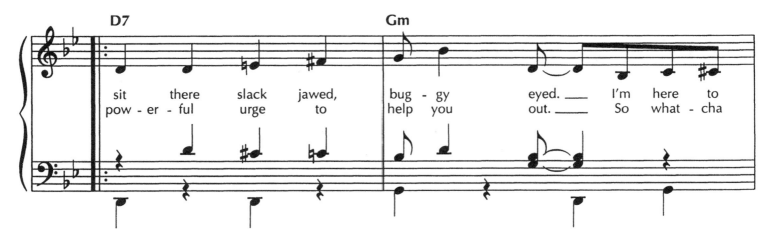

sit there slack jawed, bug - gy eyed. ___ I'm here to
pow - er - ful urge to help you out. ___ So what - cha

an - swer all your mid - day prayers. ___ You got me bo - na - fi - de
wish I real - ly want to know. ___ You got a list that's three miles

cer - ti - fied. ___ You got a ge - nie for your chargé d'af - faires. ___
long no doubt. ___ Well, all you got - ta do is rub like so. ___

___ I got a ___ And oh. _____

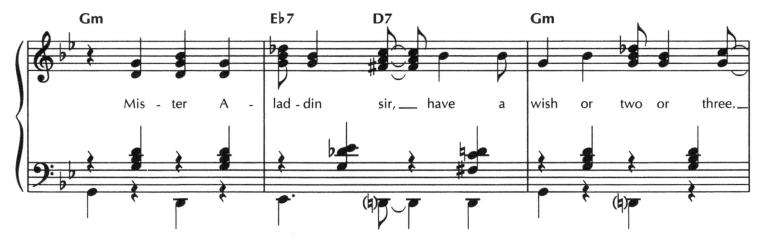

Mis - ter A - lad - din sir,__ have a wish or two or three.__

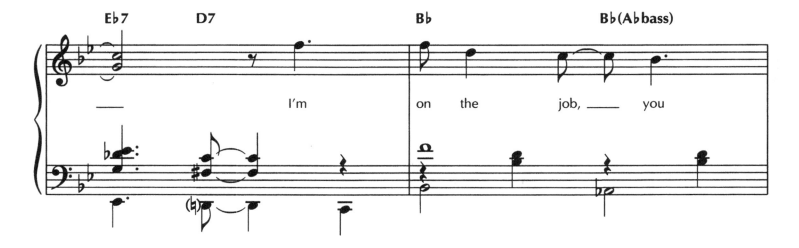

__ I'm on the job,__ you

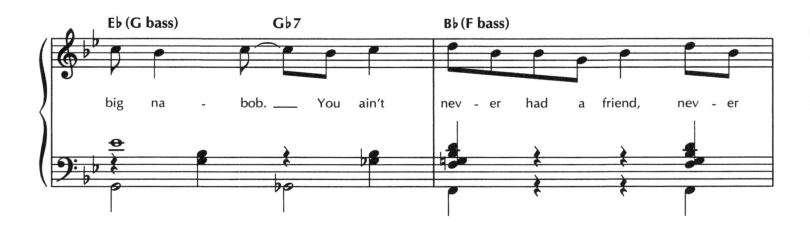

big na - bob.__ You ain't nev - er had a friend, nev - er

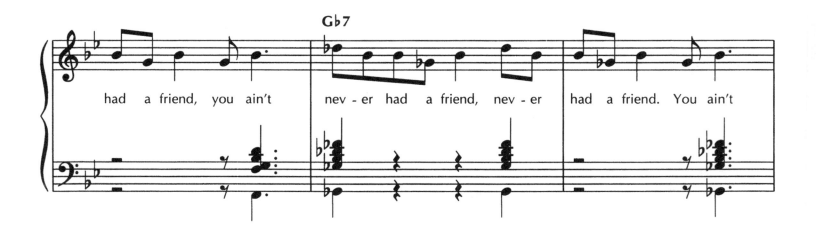

had a friend, you ain't nev - er had a friend, nev - er had a friend. You ain't

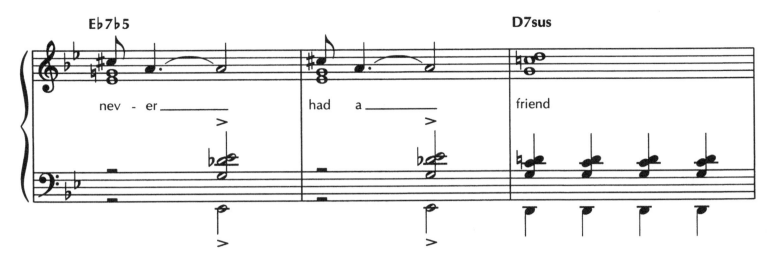

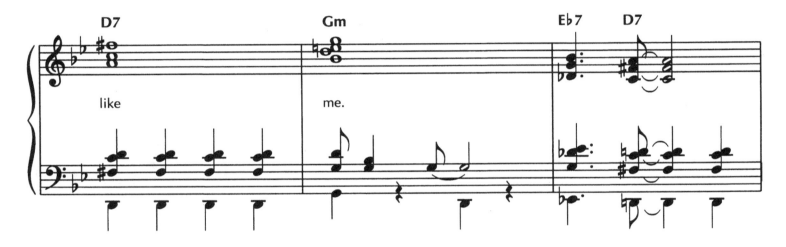

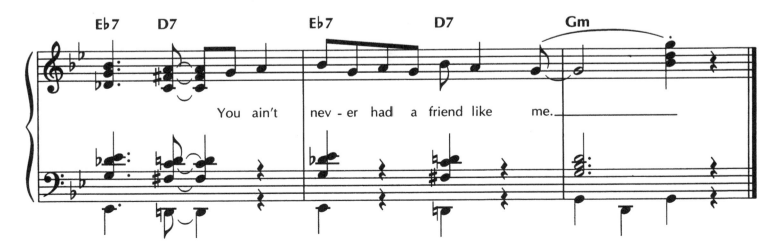

God Help the Outcasts

from Walt Disney's THE HUNCHBACK OF NOTRE DAME

Electronic Organs
Upper: Brass 8', Clarinet 8'
Lower: Strings 8',4'
Pedal: String Bass
Vib./Trem.: On, Fast

Drawbar Organs
Upper: 82 5864 200
Lower: (00) 7103 000
Pedal: String Bass
Vib./Trem.: On, Fast

Music by ALAN MENKEN
Lyrics by STEPHEN SCHWARTZ

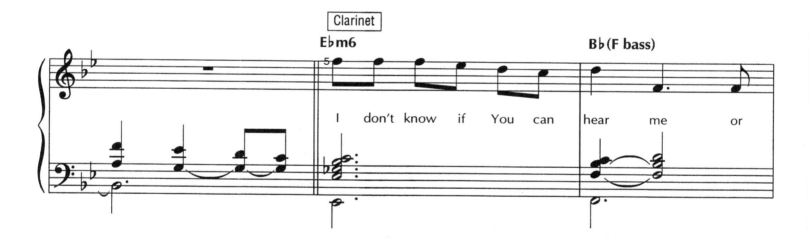

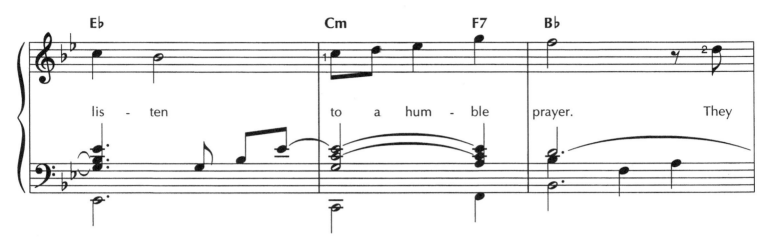

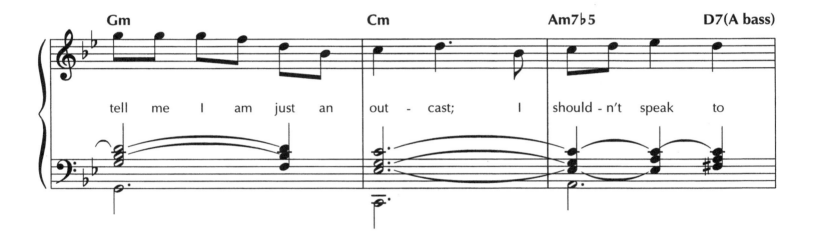

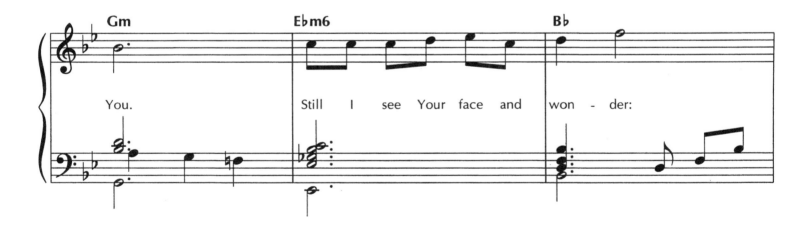

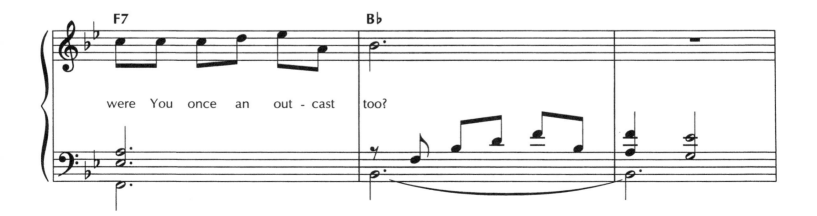

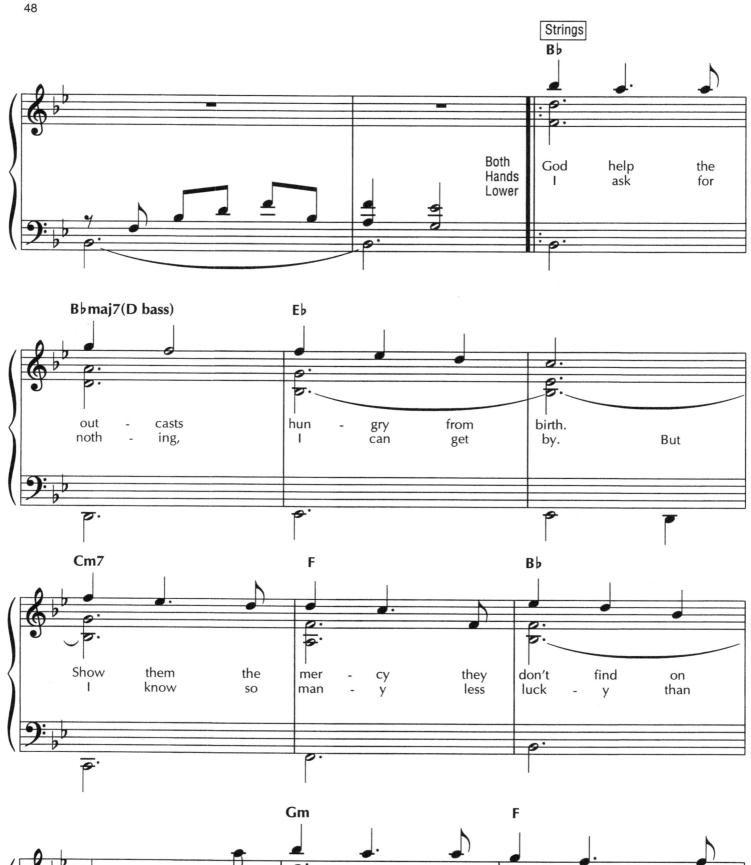

Strings
B♭

Both Hands Lower

God help the
I ask for

B♭maj7(D bass)   E♭

out - casts   hun - gry from   birth.
noth - ing,   I - can get   by.   But

Cm7   F   B♭

Show them the mer - cy they   don't find on
I know so man - y less   luck - y than

Gm   F

earth.   The lost and for - got - ten,   they
I.   God help the out - casts,   the

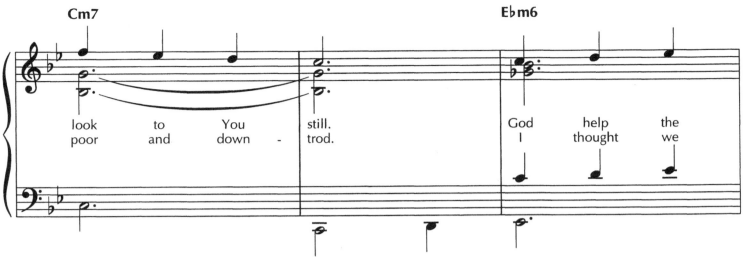

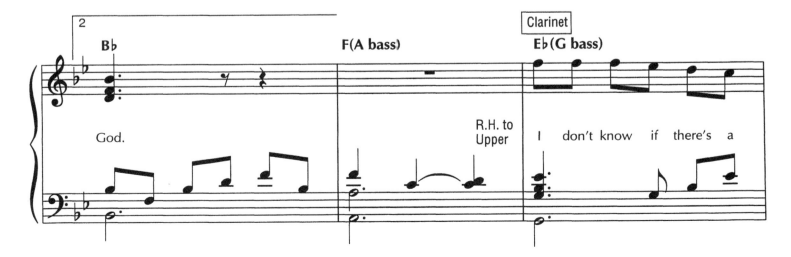

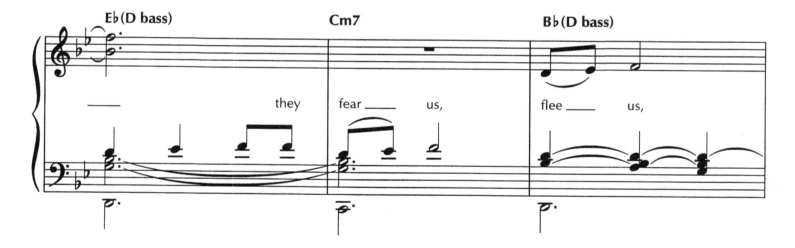

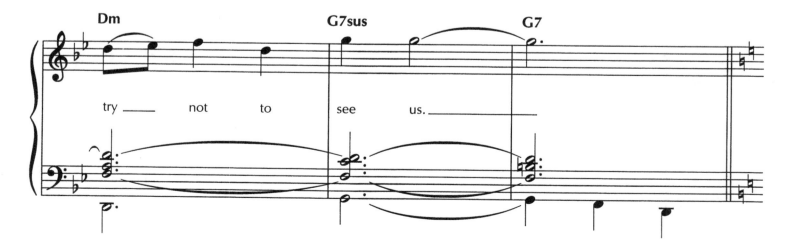

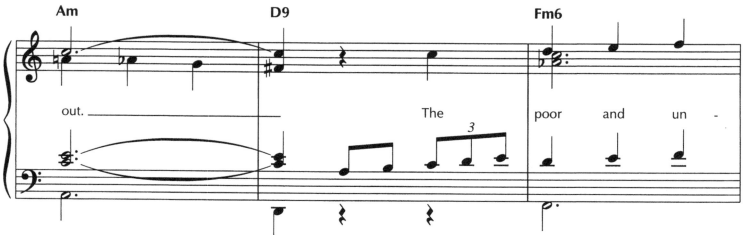

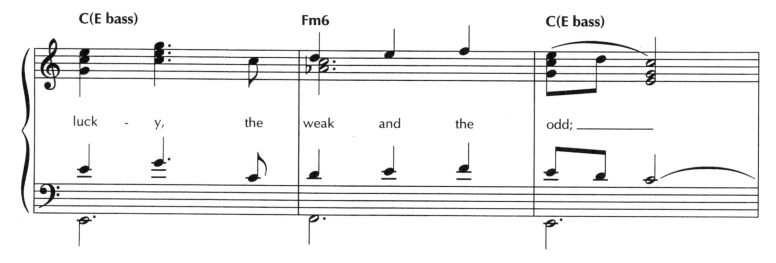

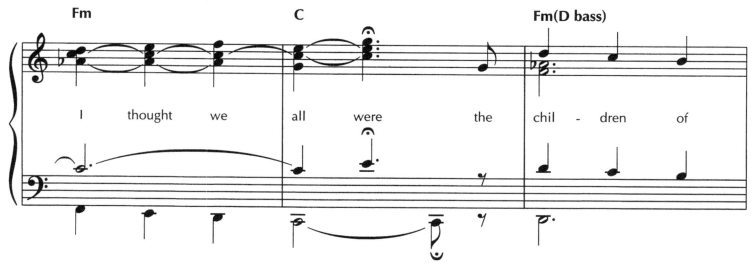

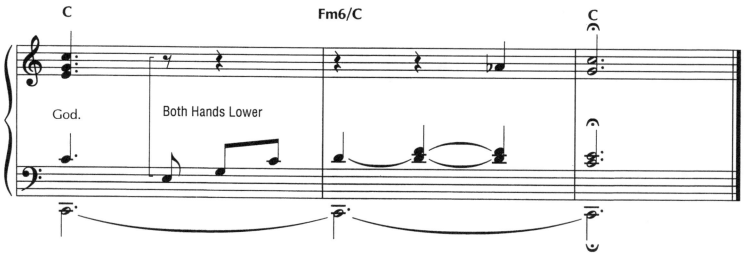

It's a Small World
from Disneyland Resort® and Magic Kingdom® Park

Electronic and Pipe Organs

Upper: Trumpet (or Brass) 8'
Lower: Flutes 8', 4', String 8', Reed 4'
Pedal: 16', 8' Sustain
Trem: On – Full
Automatic Rhythm: March

Drawbar Organs

Upper: 00 6787 654 (00)
Lower: (00) 7654 332 (0)
Pedal: 5 (0) 5 (0) (Spinet 5)
      String Bass
Vibrato: On – Full
Automatic Rhythm: March

Words and Music by RICHARD M. SHERMAN
and ROBERT B. SHERMAN

March tempo

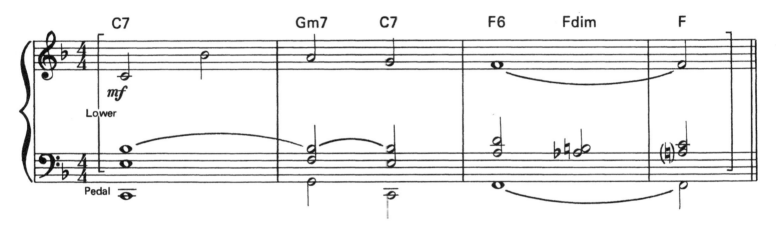

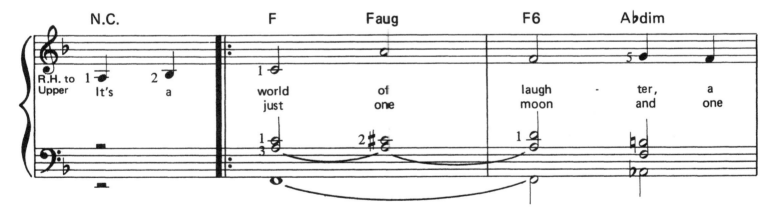

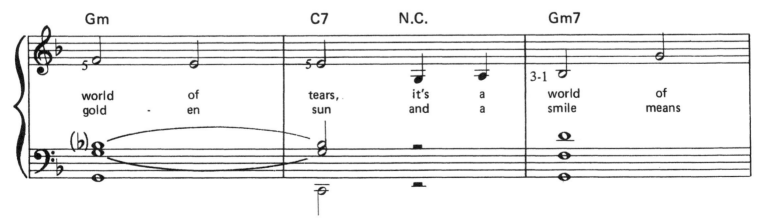

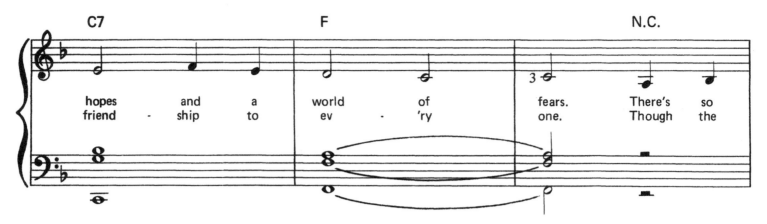

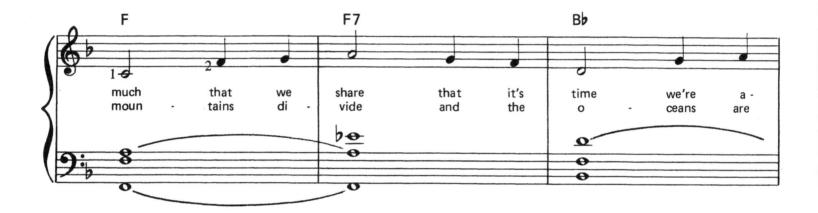

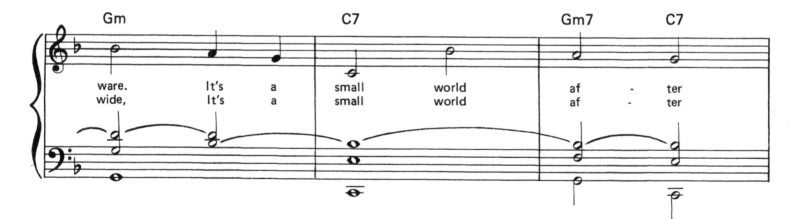

Upper $\{$ 60 6787 654 (00) / Add 16' $\}$ *(2nd time – 8va to end)*

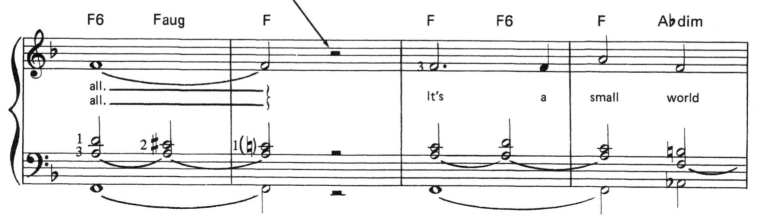

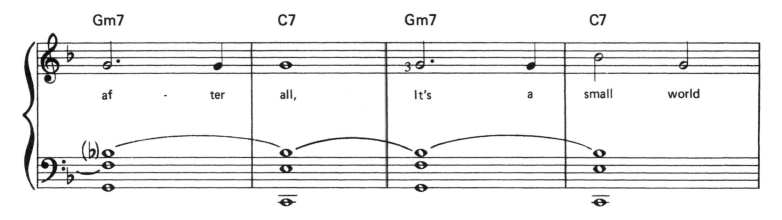

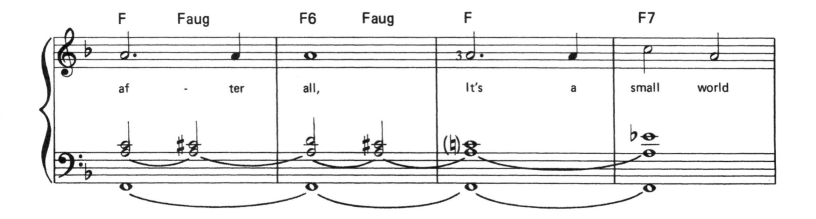

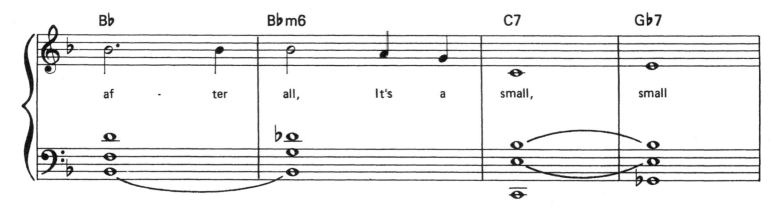

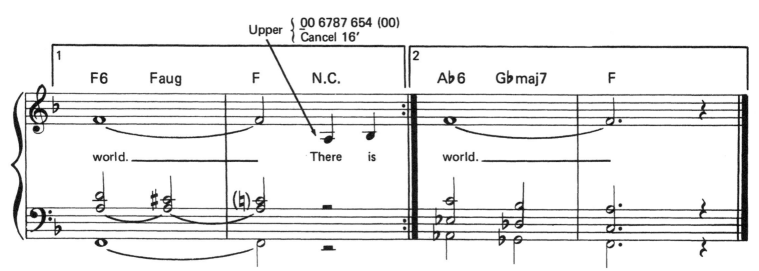

Once Upon a Dream
from Walt Disney's SLEEPING BEAUTY

Electronic and Pipe Organs

Upper: Flutes (or Tibias) 16', 8'
          Strings 8', 4'
Lower: Diapason 8', Flute 4'
Pedal: 16', 8' Sustain
Trem: On – Full
Automatic Rhythm: Waltz

Drawbar Organs

Upper: 60 0805 555 (00)
Lower: (00) 6544 321 (0)
Pedal: 5 (0) 5 (0) (Spinet 5)
          String Bass
Vibrato: On – Full
Automatic Rhythm: Waltz

Words and Music by SAMMY FAIN and
JACK LAWRENCE
Adapted from a Theme by TCHAIKOVSKY

Moderately

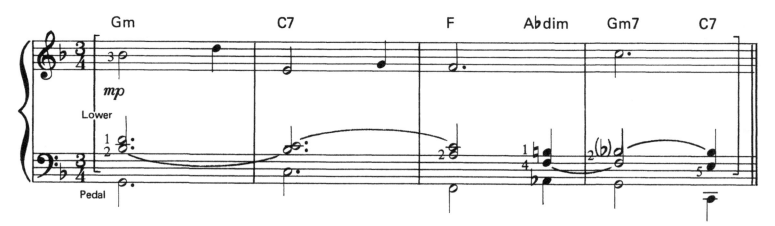

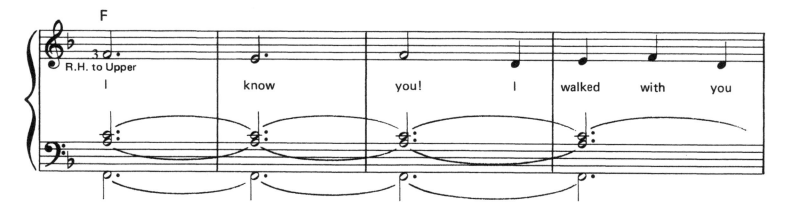

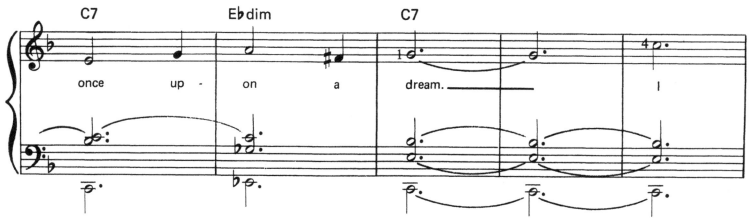

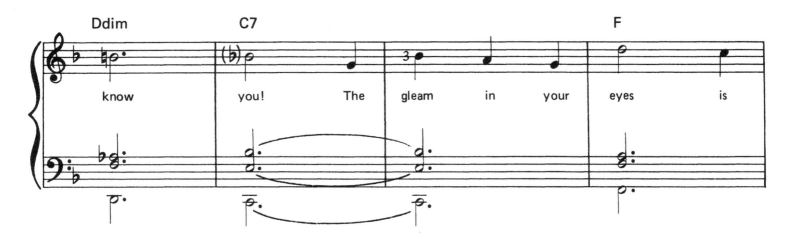

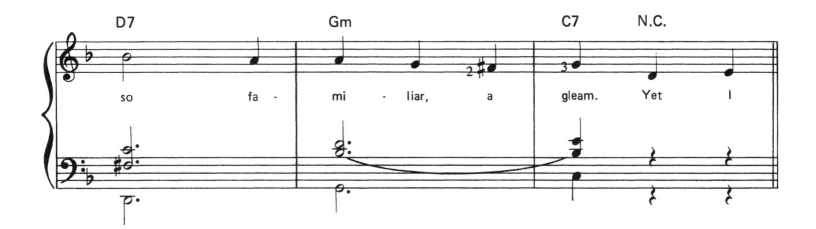

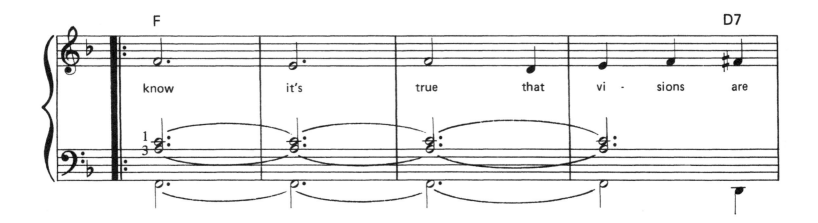

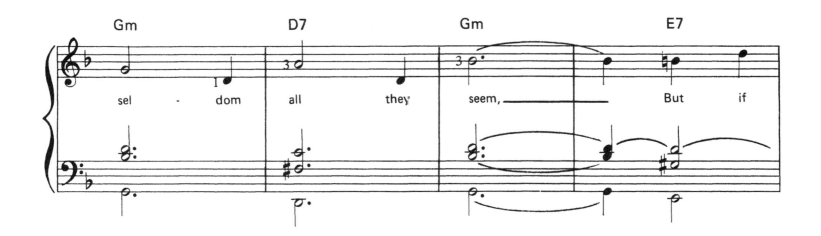

58

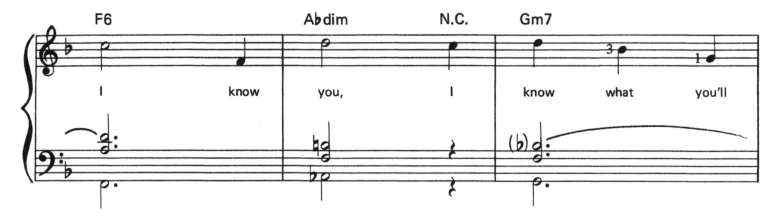

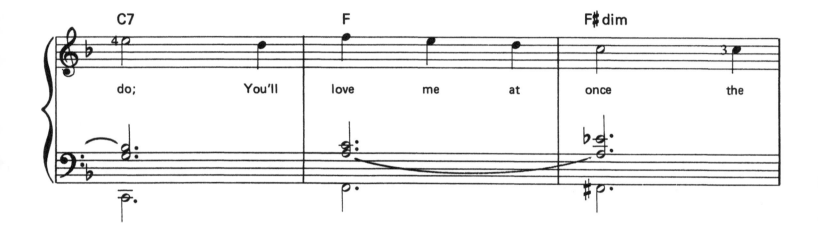

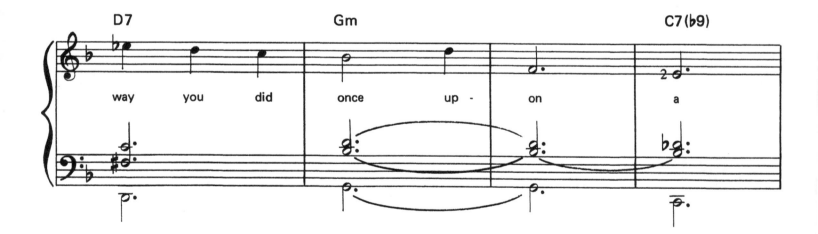

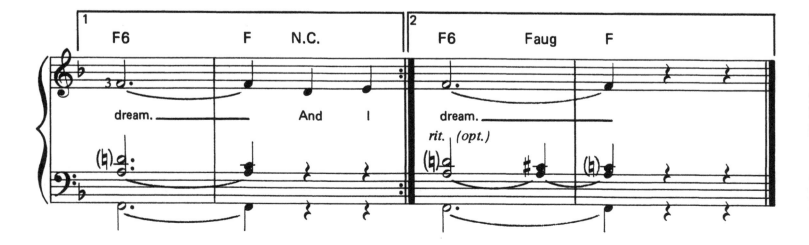

Supercalifragilisticexpialidocious

from Walt Disney's MARY POPPINS

Electronic and Pipe Organs

Upper: Flutes (or Tibias) 16', 4', 1'
Lower: Diapason 8'
       String 4'
Pedal: 16', 8' Sustain
Trem: On — Full
Automatic Rhythm: Swing

Drawbar Organs

Upper: 60 0800 008 (00)
Lower: (00) 5433 323 (0)
Pedal: 5 (0) 5 (0) (Spinet 5)
       String Bass
Vibrato: On — Full
Automatic Rhythm: Swing

Words and Music by RICHARD M. SHERMAN
and ROBERT B. SHERMAN

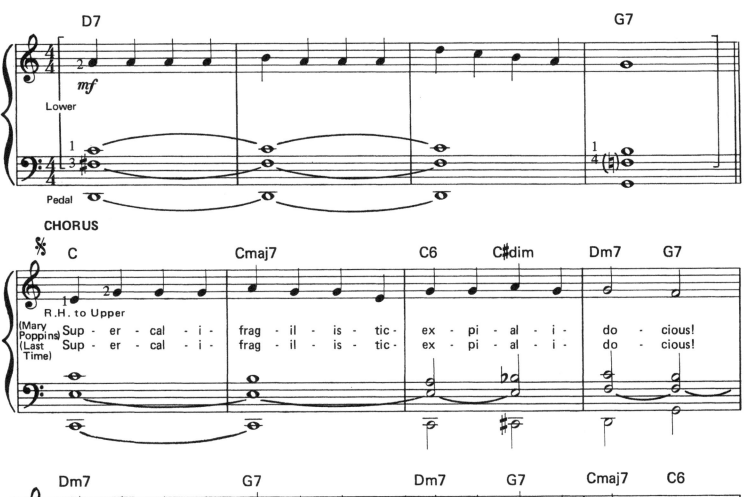

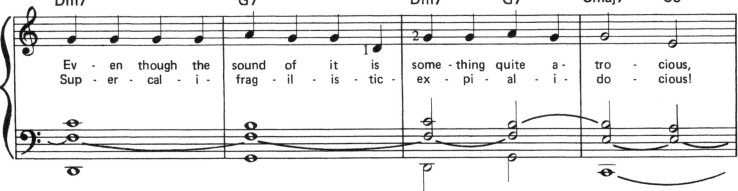

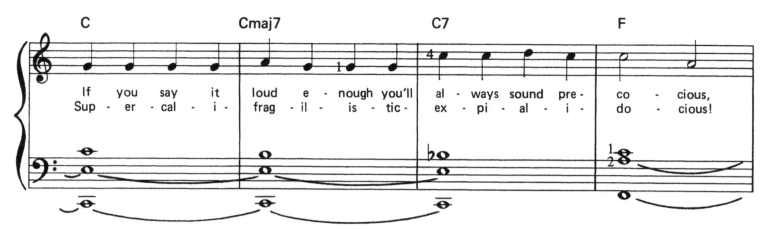

C   **Cmaj7**   **C7**   **F**

If you say it loud e - nough you'll al - ways sound pre - co - cious,
Sup - er - cal - i - frag - il - is - tic - ex - pi - al - i - do - cious!

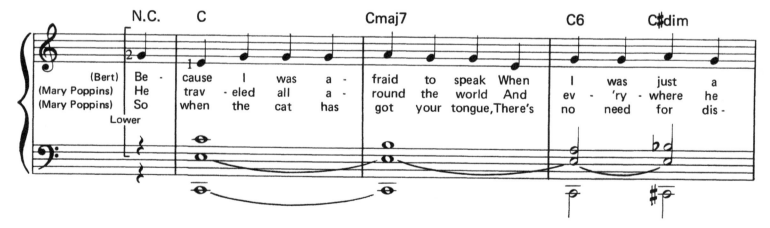

To Coda (Last Time)

F6   **E♭dim**   **C**   **C♯dim**   ⊕ **Dm7**   **G7**   **C**

Sup - er - cal - i - frag - il - is - tic - ex - pi - al - i - do - cious!
Sup - er - cal - i - frag - il - is - tic -

VERSE

N.C.   **C**   **Cmaj7**   **C6**   **C♯dim**

(Bert) Be - cause I was a - fraid to speak When I was just a
(Mary Poppins) He trav - eled all a - round the world And ev - 'ry - where he
(Mary Poppins) So when the cat has got your tongue, There's no need for dis -

Lower

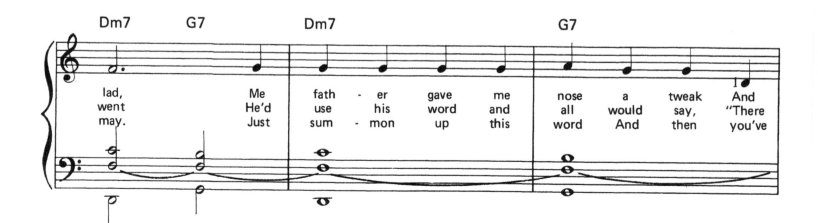

Dm7   **G7**   **Dm7**   **G7**

lad, Me fath - er gave me nose a tweak And
went He'd use his word and all would say, "There
may. Just sum - mon up this word And then you've

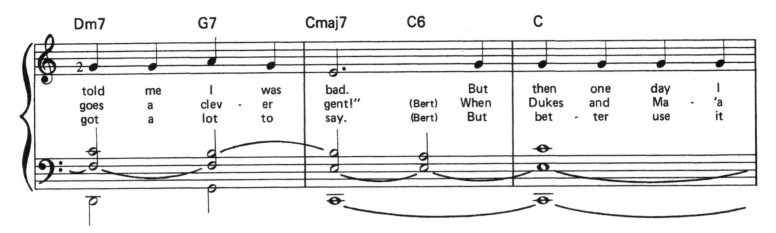

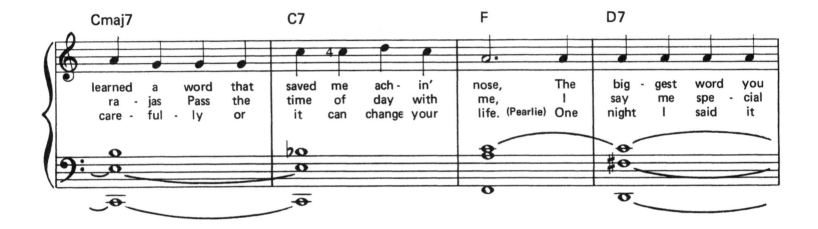

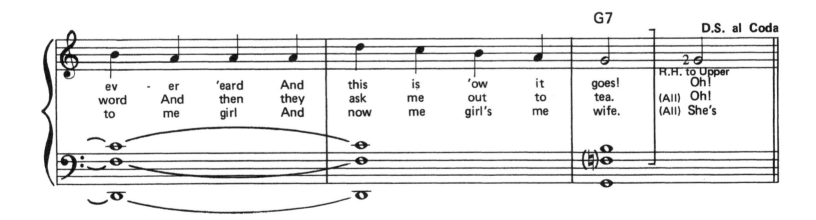

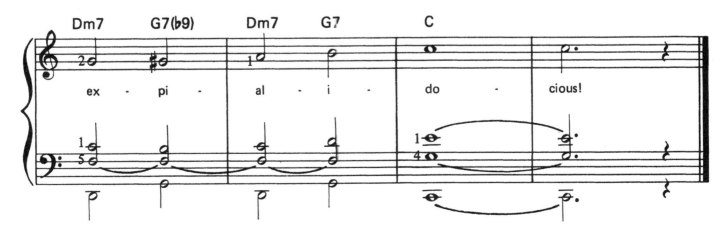

When You Wish Upon a Star
from Walt Disney's PINOCCHIO

Electronic Organs
Upper: Flutes (or Tibias) 16′, 8′, 4′, 2′
       String 8′
Lower: Flutes 8′, 4′
Pedal: 16′, 8′
Vib./Trem.: On, Slow

Drawbar Organs
Upper: 80 8104 103
Lower: (00) 6303 004
Pedal: 25
Vib./Trem.: On, Slow

Words by NED WASHINGTON
Music by LEIGH HARLINE

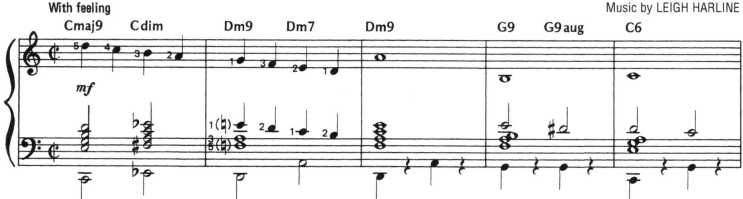

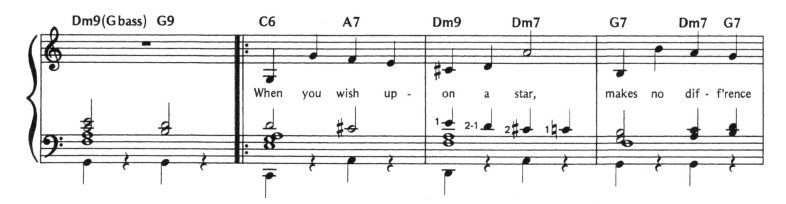

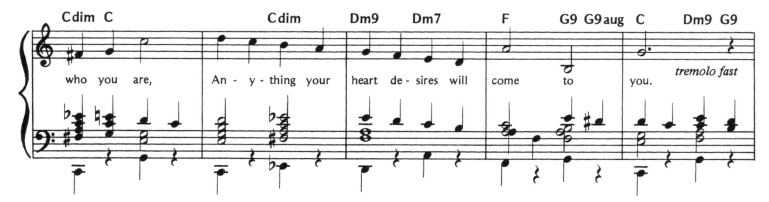

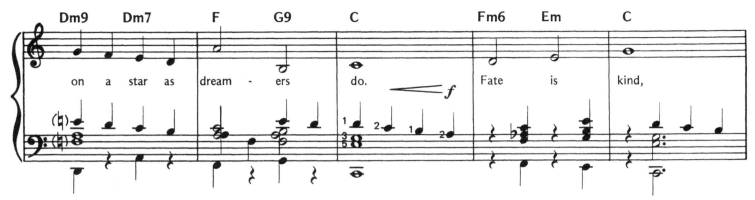

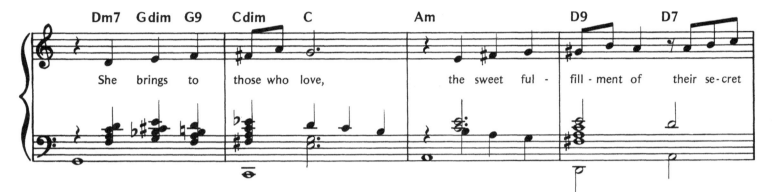

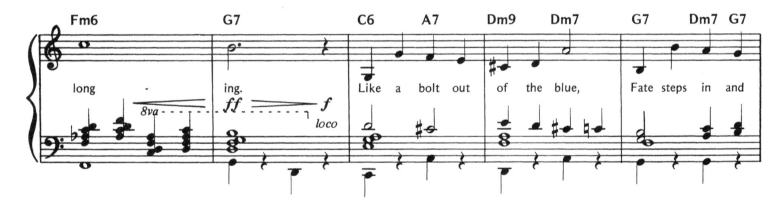

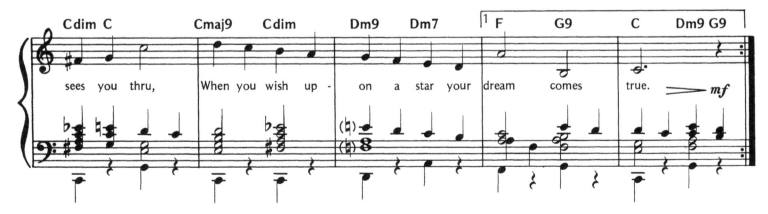

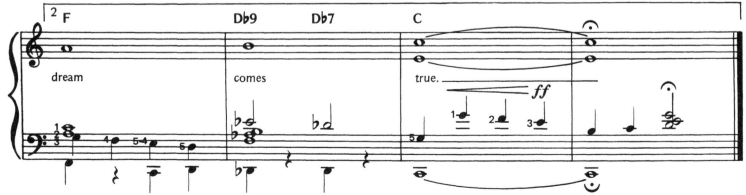

A Whole New World
from Walt Disney's ALADDIN

Electronic Organs
Upper: Oboe 8'
Lower: Piano (Med. sustain)
Pedal: Bass 8'
Vib./Trem.: Off

Drawbar Organs
Upper: 08 00800 002
Lower: Preset Piano or
     (00) 7400 000
Pedals: 25
Vib./Trem.: Off

Music by ALAN MENKEN
Lyrics by TIM RICE

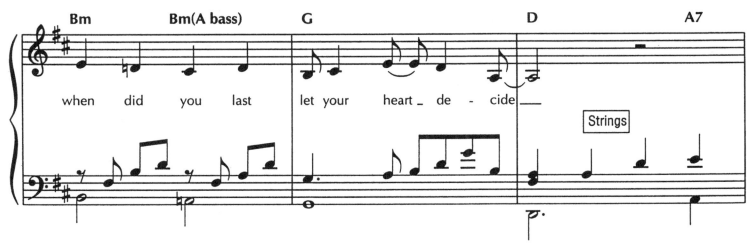

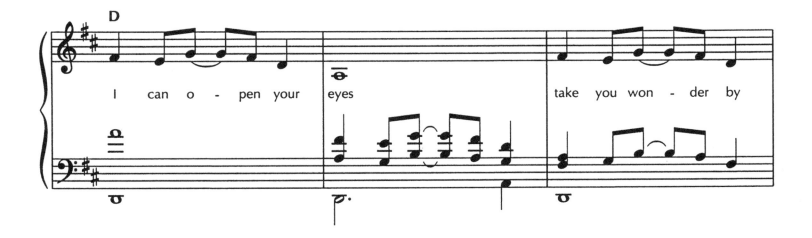

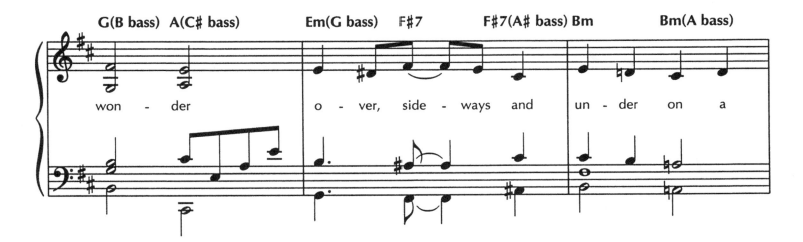

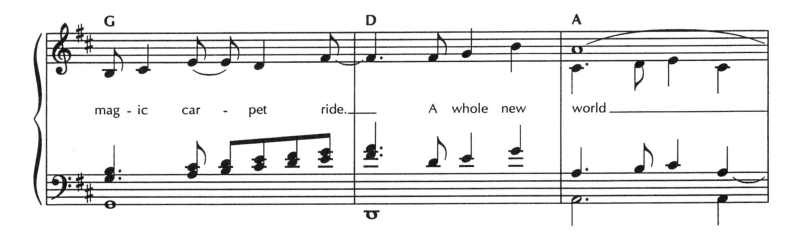

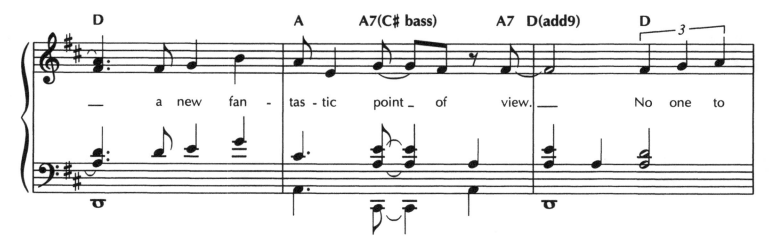

a new fan-tas-tic point of view. No one to

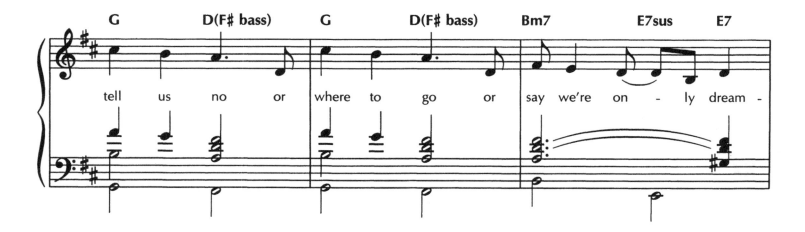

tell us no or where to go or say we're on-ly dream-

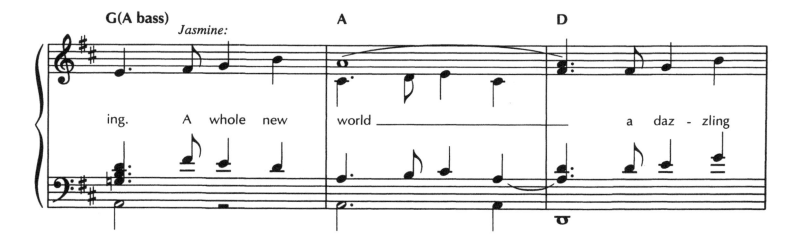

Jasmine:

ing. A whole new world a daz-zling

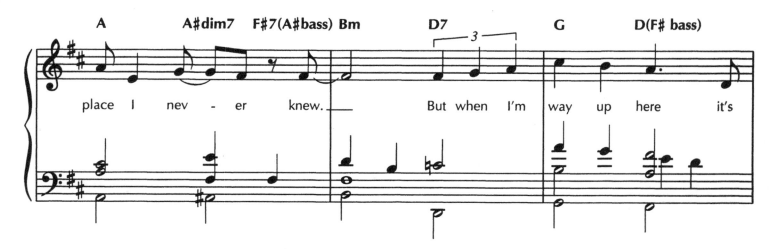

place I nev-er knew. But when I'm way up here it's

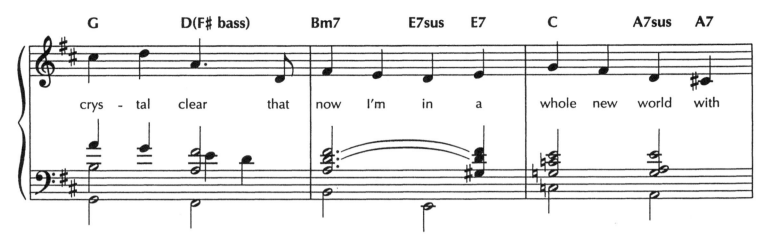

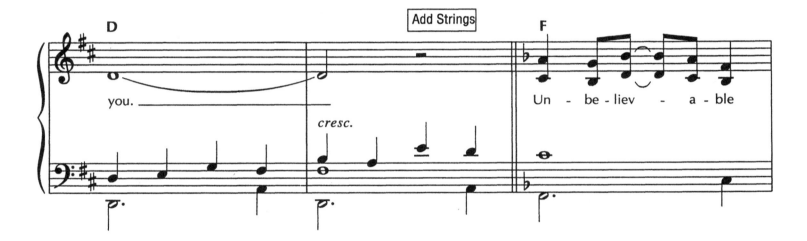

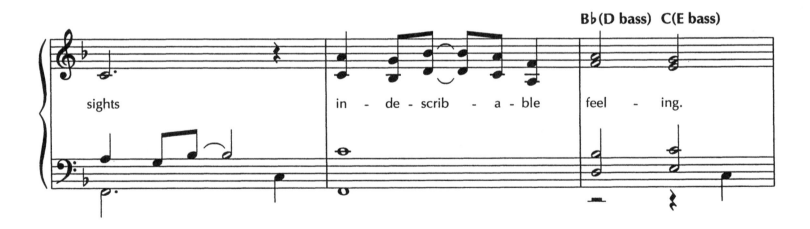

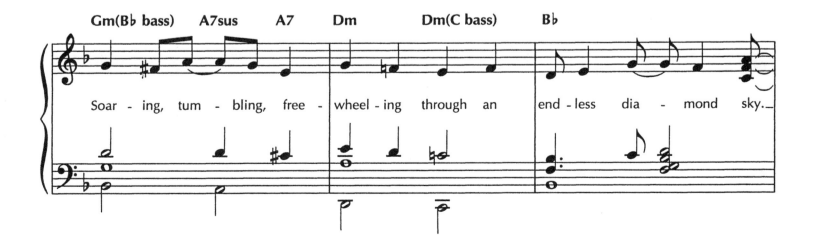

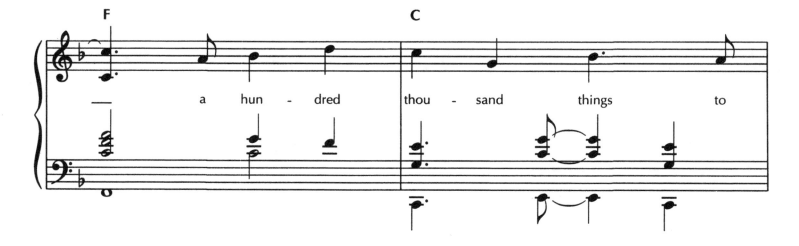

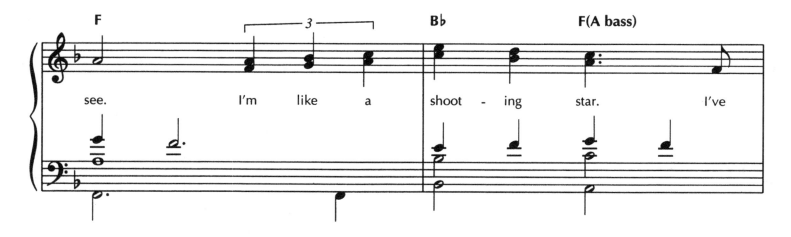

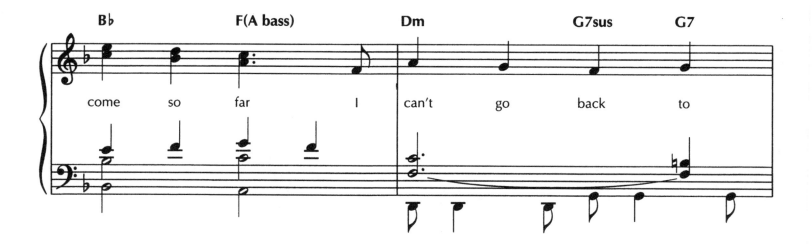

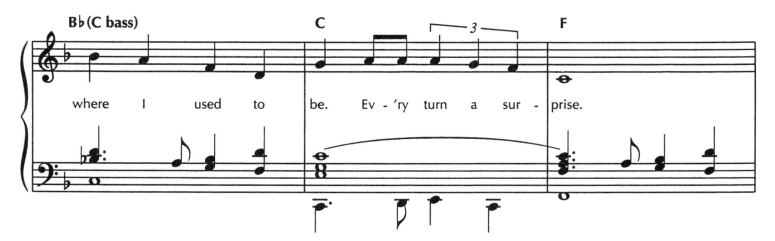

where I used to be. Ev - 'ry turn a sur - prise.

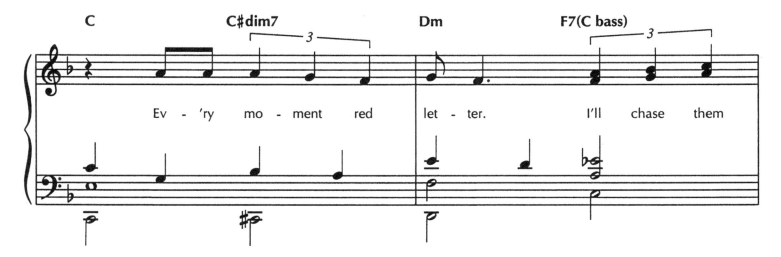

Ev - 'ry mo - ment red let - ter. I'll chase them

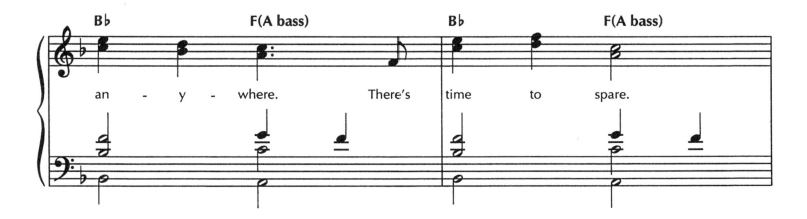

an - y - where. There's time to spare.

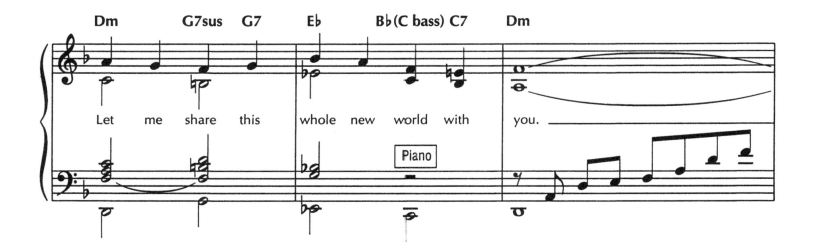

Let me share this whole new world with you.

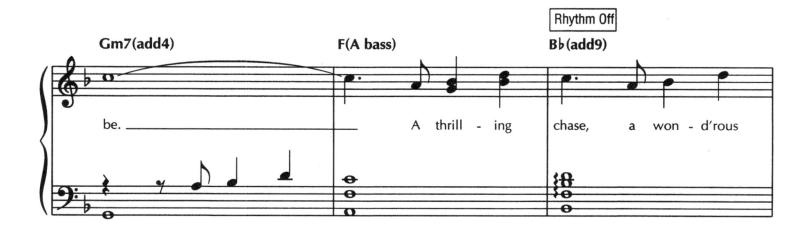

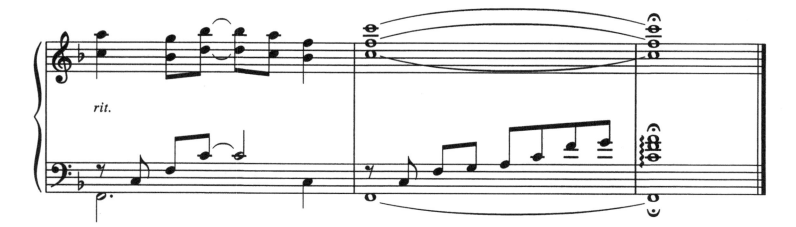

You'll Be in My Heart

(Pop Version)
from Walt Disney Pictures' TARZAN™

Electronic Organs
Upper: Flute (or Tibia) 4'
      Clarinet 8'
Lower: Strings 8', 4'
Pedal: 16', 8'
Vib./Trem.: On, Fast

Drawbar Organs
Upper: 53 5864 101
Lower: (00) 7104 000
Pedal: 35
Vib./Trem.: On, Fast

Words and Music by
PHIL COLLINS

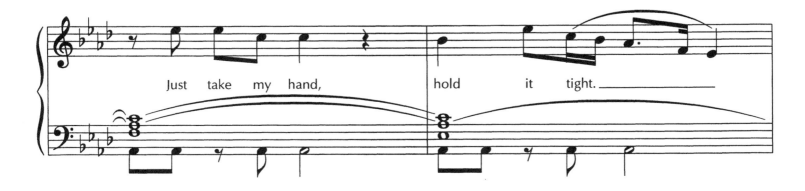

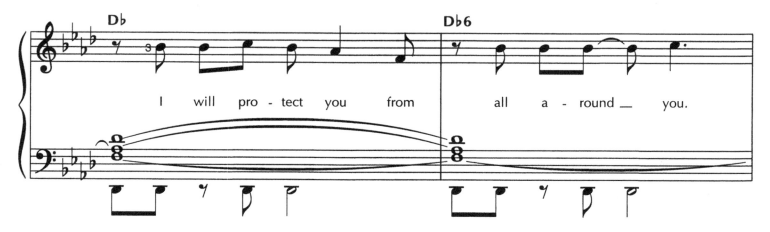

I will pro- tect you from all a - round __ you.

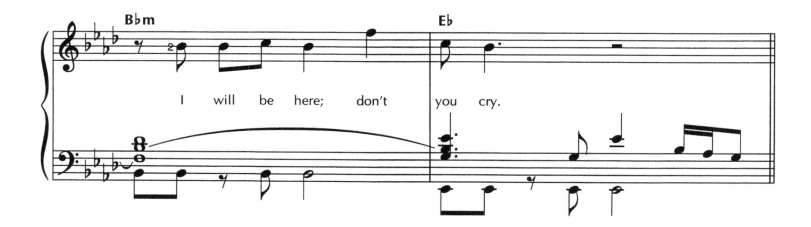

I will be here; don't you cry.

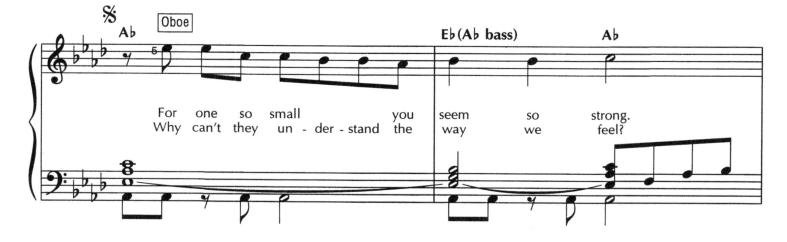

For one so small you seem so strong.
Why can't they un - der - stand the way we feel?

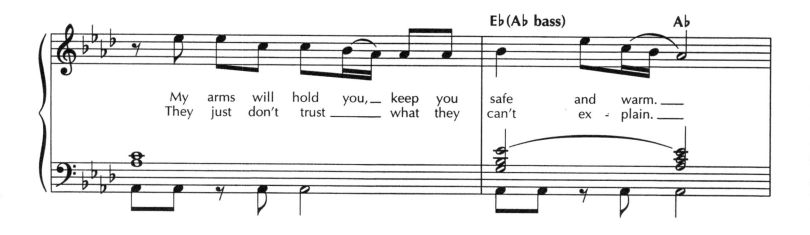

My arms will hold you, __ keep you safe and warm. __
They just don't trust _____ what they can't ex - plain. __

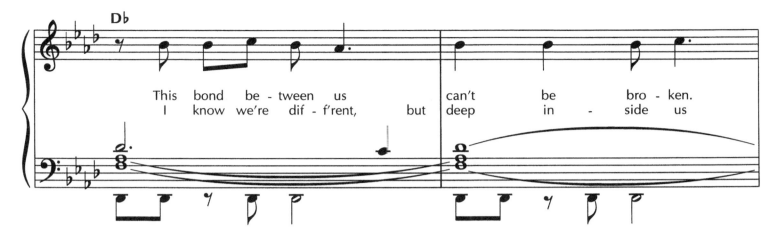

This bond be-tween us
I know we're dif-f'rent, but

can't be bro-ken.
deep in - side us

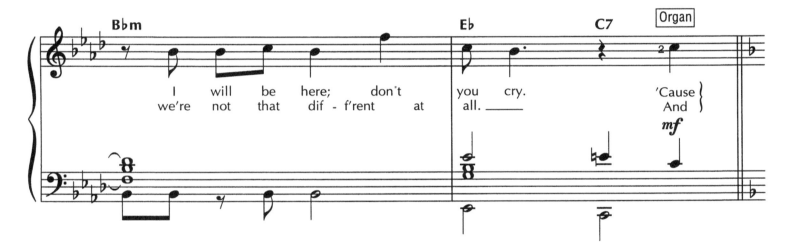

I will be here; don't
we're not that dif - f'rent at

you cry.
all.____

'Cause
And

you'll be in ____ my ____ heart, yes,

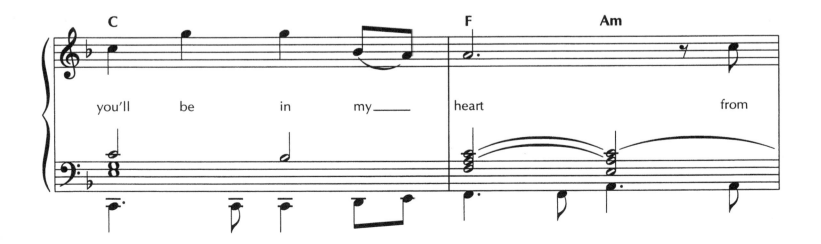

you'll be in my ____ heart

from

To Coda ⊕

this day on now and for - ev - er - more_____

You'll be in _____ my ___ heart no

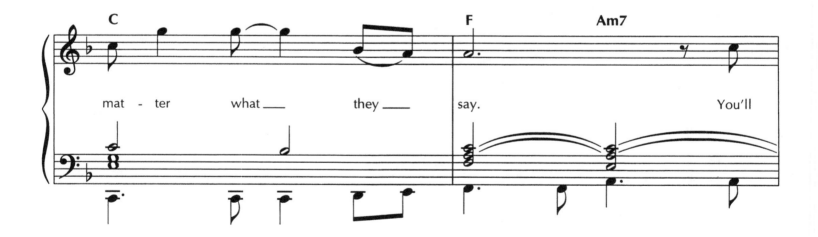

mat - ter what ___ they ___ say. You'll

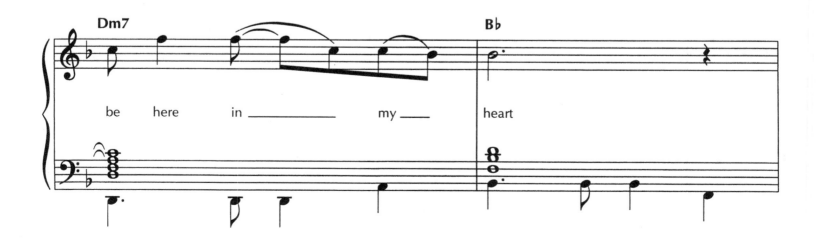

be here in _____ my ___ heart

75

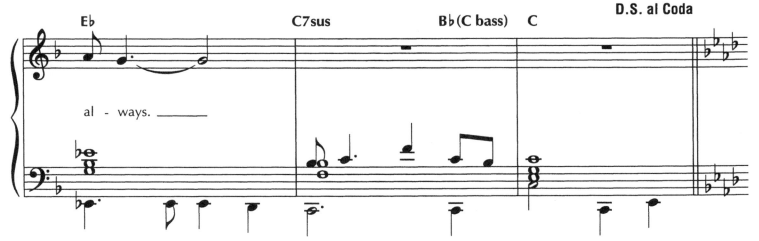

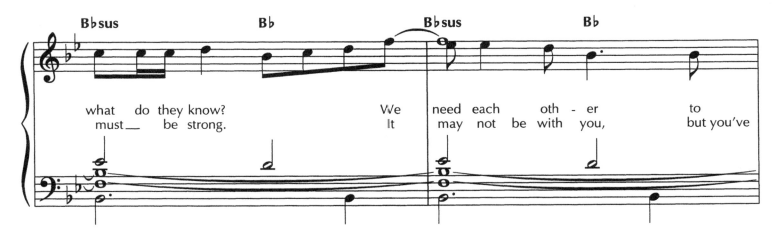

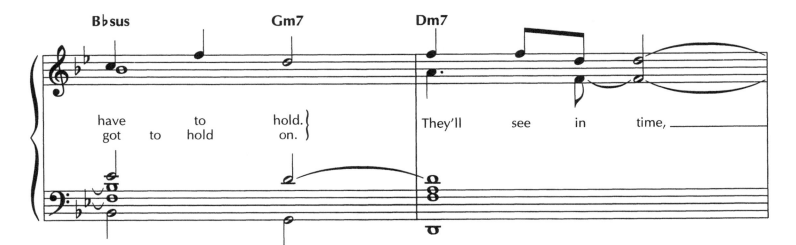

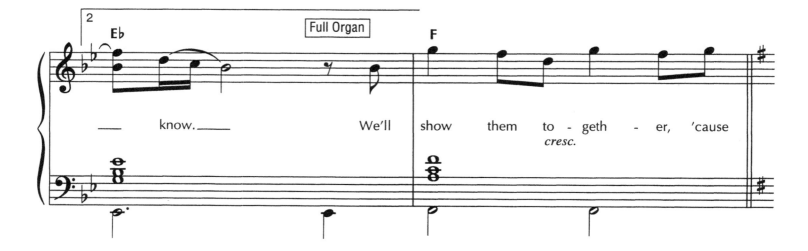

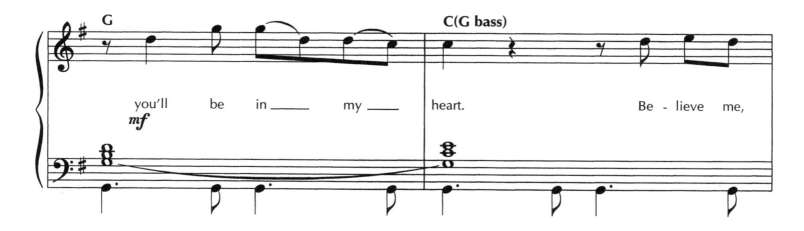

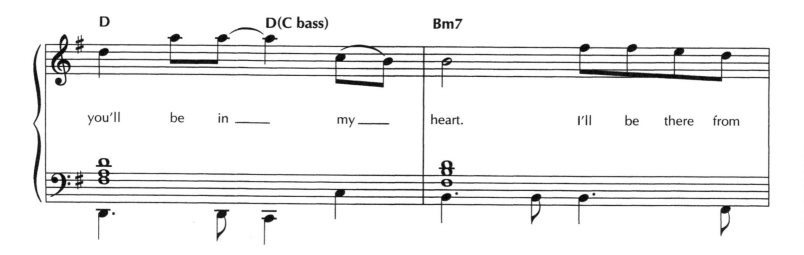

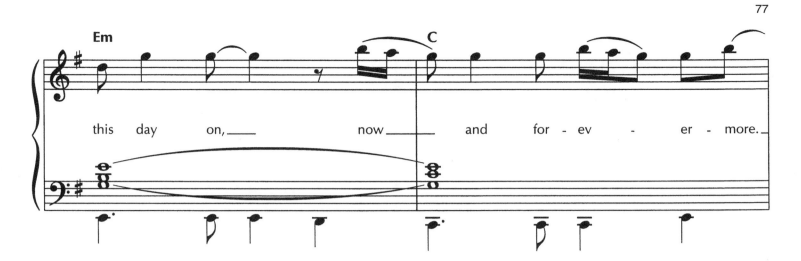

this day on,___ now___ and for - ev - er - more.

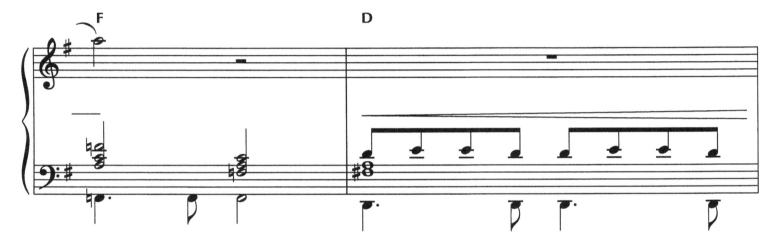

You'll be in ___ my ___ heart (You'll be here ___ in my heart.) no

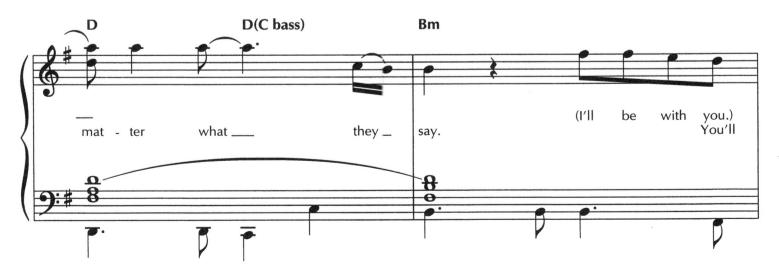

mat - ter what ___ they _ say. (I'll be with you.) You'll

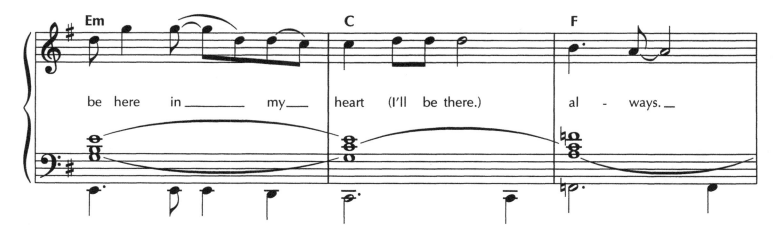

be here in _____ my ___ heart (I'll be there.) al - ways. __

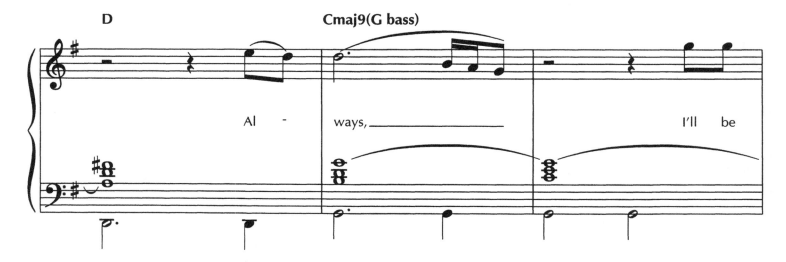

Al - ways, _____ I'll be

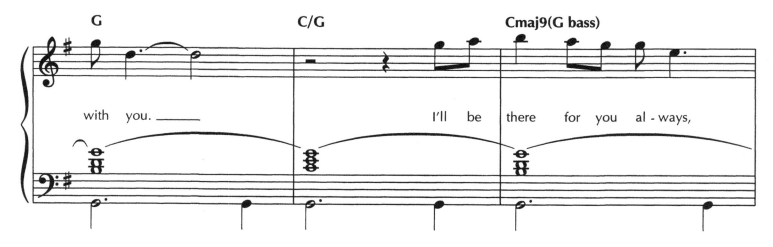

with you. _____ I'll be there for you al - ways,

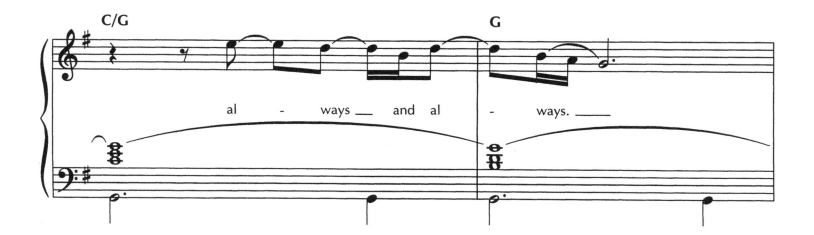

al - ways __ and al - ways. ___

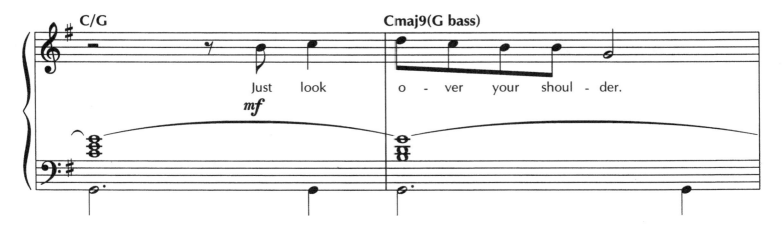

Just look o - ver your shoul - der.

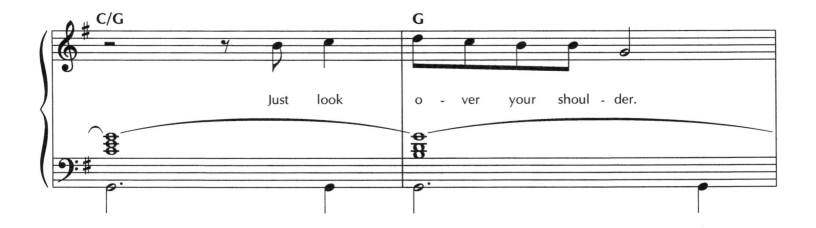

Just look o - ver your shoul - der.

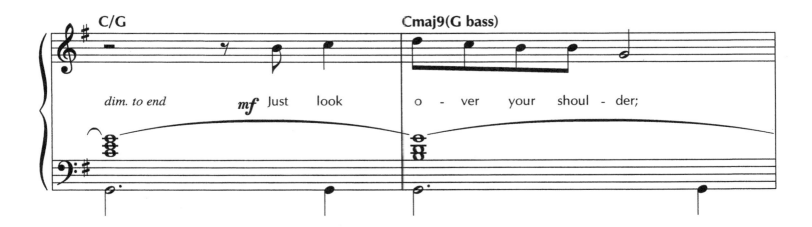

dim. to end *mf* Just look o - ver your shoul - der;

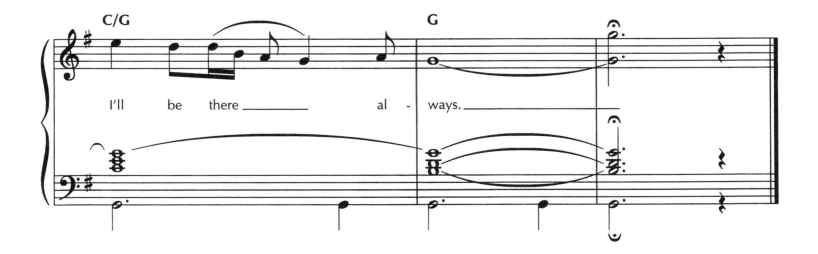

I'll be there _____ al - ways. _____

FOR ORGANS, PIANOS & ELECTRONIC KEYBOARDS

E-Z PLAY® TODAY PUBLICATIONS

The E-Z Play® Today songbook series is the shortest distance between beginning music and playing fun!
Check out this list of highlights and visit halleonard.com for a complete listing of all volumes and songlists.

HAL•LEONARD®

Prices, contents and availability
subject to change without notice

0421
330